# *Improving Non-fiction Writing at Key Stages 1 & 2: the Success Approach*

# IMPROVING LITERACY: CREATIVE APPROACHES

# *Improving Non-fiction Writing at Key Stages 1 & 2: the Success Approach*

## Margaret McNeil and Alan Peat

Nash Pollock
Publishing

© Margaret McNeil and Alan Peat

First published 2004

Published by
Nash Pollock Publishing
32 Warwick Street
Oxford OX4 1SX

10  9  8  7  6  5  4  3  2  1

*Orders to:*
York Publishing Services
64 Hallfield Road
Layerthorpe
York  YO31 7ZQ

A catalogue record of this book is available from the British Library.

ISBN: 1 898255 44 X

Design and typesetting by Black Dog Design, Buckingham
Printed in Great Britain by The Cromwell Press, Wiltshire

# Contents

## Acknowledgements and dedication

The publication of this book would not have been possible without the help of a number of individuals. We are especially grateful for the helpful comments and support we have received from James Nash who helped us shape the book into its present form.

We would also like to thank the schools, teachers and pupils who worked with us trying out the SUCCESS Approach, in particular Holy Trinity School in Blackburn with Darwen; Ewyas Harold School, Herefordshire; Littlemoor School in Oldham; and Stalyhill County Junior School, Tameside.

We dedicate the book to Derek with our love – we could not have managed it without his patience, cooking skills and provision of coffee and wine when needed.

# National Literacy Strategy Framework links

| NLS Links | Content | Location |
|---|---|---|
| YEAR 1 TERM 1 | | |
| T16 | Write and draw simple instructions and labels for everyday classroom use, e.g. in role play area, for equipment | Chapter 1 |
| YEAR 1 TERM 2 | | |
| T25 | Assemble information from own experience, e.g. food, pets; use simple sentences to describe, based on examples from reading | Chapter 2 |
| | write simple non-chronological reports; organise in lists, separate pages, charts | Chapter 4 |
| YEAR 1 TERM 3 | | |
| T20 | Write simple recounts linked to topics of interest/study or to personal experience, using the language of texts read as models for own writing. Make group/class books, e.g. *our day at school, our trip to ...* | Chapter 2 |
| YEAR 2 TERM 1 | | |
| T15 | Write simple instructions, e.g getting to school, playing a game | Chapter 1 |
| T16 | Use models from reading to organise instructions sequentially, e.g. listing points in order, each point depending on the previous one, numbering | Chapter 1 |
| T17 | Use diagrams in instructions, e.g. drawing and labelling diagrams as part of a set of instructions | Chapter 1 |
| T18 | Use appropriate register in writing instructions, i.e. direct, impersonal, building on texts read | Chapter 1 |
| YEAR 2 TERM 2 | | |
| T21 | Produce simple flow charts or diagrams that explain a process | Chapter 3 |
| YEAR 2 TERM 3 | | |
| T20 | Write non-fiction texts, using texts read as models for own writing, e.g. use of headings, sub-headings, captions | Chapter 2 |

|  |  |  |
|---|---|---|
| T21 | Write non-chronological reports based on structure of known texts, e.g. *There are two sorts of x ...; they live in x ....; the A's have x ..., but the B's etc.*, using appropriate language to present, sequence and categorise ideas | Chapter 4 |

### YEAR 3 TERM 1

|  |  |  |
|---|---|---|
| T21 | Make a simple record of information from texts read, e.g. by completing a chart of information discovered, by listing keywords, drawing together notes from more than one source | Chapter 4 |
| T22 | Write simple non-chronological reports from known information e.g. from own experience or from texts read, using notes to organise and present ideas. Write for a known audience, e.g. other pupils in class, teacher, parent | Chapter 4 |

### YEAR 3 TERM 2

|  |  |  |
|---|---|---|
| T16 | Write instructions e.g. rules for games, recipes, using a range of organisational devices, e.g. lists, dashes, commas for lists in sentences, recognising the importance of correct sequence; use 'writing frames' as appropriate for support | Chapter 1 |

### YEAR 3 TERM 3

|  |  |  |
|---|---|---|
| T22 | Experiment with recounting the same event in a variety of ways e.g. in the form of a story, a letter, a news report | Chapter 5 |

### YEAR 4 TERM 1

|  |  |  |
|---|---|---|
| T27 | Write a non-chronological report, including the use of organisational devices, e.g. numbered lists, headings for conciseness by generalising some of the details, deleting the least important details | Chapter 4 |

### YEAR 4 TERM 2

|  |  |  |
|---|---|---|
| T24 | Improve the cohesion of written explanations through paragraphing and the use of link phrases and organisational devices such as sub-headings and numbering | Chapter 3 |
| T25 | Write explanations of a process, using conventions identified through reading | Chapter 3 |

## YEAR 4 TERM 3

| T21 | Assemble and sequence points in order to plan the presentation of a point of view, e.g. on hunting, school rules | Chapter 6 |

| T23 | Present a point of view in writing, e.g. in the form of a letter, a report or a script, linking points persuasively and selecting style and vocabulary appropriate to the reader | Chapter 6 |

## YEAR 5 TERM 1

| T24 | Write recounts based on subject, topic or personal experiences for (a) a close friend and (b) an unknown reader, e.g. an account of a field trip, a match, a historical event | Chapter 2 |

| T25 | Write instructional texts, and test them out, e.g. instructions for loading computers, design briefs for technology, rules for games | Chapter 1 |

## YEAR 5 TERM 2

| T22 | Plan, compose, edit and refine short non-chronological reports and explanatory texts, using reading as a source, focusing on clarity, conciseness and impersonal style | Chapter 4 |

| T23 | Record and acknowledge sources in their own writing | Chapter 4 |

## YEAR 5 TERM 3

| T19 | Construct an argument in note form or full text to persuade others of a point of view and:<br>– present the case to the class or a group<br>– evaluate its effectiveness | Chapter 6 |

## YEAR 6 TERM 1

| T14 | Develop the skills of biographical and autobiographical writing in role | Chapter 2 |

| T15 | Develop a journalistic style through considering:<br>– balanced and ethical reporting<br>– what is of public interest in events<br>– the interest of the reader<br>– selection and presentation of information | Chapter 5 |

| T16 | Use the styles and conventions of journalism to report on real or imaginary events | Chapter 5 |

| T17 | Write non-chronological reports linked to other subjects | Chapter 4 |

T18    Construct effective arguments:                              Chapter 6
       – developing a point of view logically and
         effectively
       – supporting and illustrating points persuasively
       – anticipating possible objections
       – harnessing the known views, interests and
         feelings of the audience
       – tailoring the writing to formal presentation where
         appropriate

T19    Write a balanced report of a controversial issue:          Chapter 7
       – summarising fairly the competing views
       – analysing strengths and weaknesses of different
         positions

# Introduction

The national drive to raise writing standards has undoubtedly led teachers to encourage pupils in their classes to write more frequently. Writing more frequently does not necessarily result in writing which is effective. We have written this book to assist teachers in helping their pupils to write more effectively using a new approach – the SUCCESS Approach.

---

**THE SUCCESS APPROACH**

**Structural Understanding, Confident Composition, Self Evaluation = SUCCESS**

---

## The problems of teaching non-fiction writing

Currently the major problem which adversely affects the teaching of non-fiction forms is the lack of a common language to define the features of each form. We have asked pupils in classrooms across Britain to describe non-fiction text forms orally – in *all* instances the pupils were unable to articulate clearly how a given form is structured. Even when they were able to describe some of the language features, it was clear that an embedded understanding of text organisation did not exist.

Text organisation is of great importance when writing non-fiction and, without a consistent focus on this aspect of non-fiction writing, pupils with good ideas are not equipped with the necessary skills to organise their ideas.

In training sessions conducted nationally this lack of clarity was also evident among teachers. In more than one hundred primary schools we have asked teachers to list the sequential elements of text forms such as persuasive writing and newspaper reports. Although it was evident that teachers did have an understanding of the text forms, yet again, in *all* instances the language used to define the features was inconsistent.

Figure 1 (overleaf) is an example of the responses we received in one primary school where we asked the teachers to describe the features of a newspaper report.

As can be seen from this example, although there may be a broadly agreed structure when we teased out what the teachers meant, there was no agreed common language used. Defining a common language for describing features of each non-fiction text form is fundamentally important if we are to avoid confusion for pupils. Consistency of language allows pupils to consider the key features

| Teacher Group A | Group B | Group C | Group D |
|---|---|---|---|
| Headline | Main heading (bold) | Headline | Main heading |
| Sub-heading | | | |
| Opening statement | Opening paragraph with overview (slightly darker) | Opening statement | Opening paragraph/ sentence to explain article's content |
| Actual news | 'Story' in more detail including quotes, paragraphs | Main paragraph | Introduction paragraph – set scene |
| People's opinions | | | Another paragraph – expand one view/quotes |
| | | | Another paragraph – expand another view/quotes |
| | Concluding paragraph giving main details | Closing statement | End paragraph |

Figure 1: Teachers' descriptions of the sequential elements of a newspaper report

of each genre without having to decode new vocabulary on each subsequent occasion that the same text form is met.

The principal approach in recent years has been the use of writing frames to scaffold children's writing. Writing frames are photocopiable templates consisting of sentence starters which the pupils are expected to complete. The sentence starters are sometimes augmented with connectives and sentence modifiers such as the word 'because'.

The EXEL (Exeter Extending Literacy) project of the mid 1990s and the subsequent development of the Writing Frames/ Scaffolding approaches to non-fiction text writing undoubtedly had a major impact on teachers' understanding, and pupils' writing, of non-fiction forms. As Maureen Lewis and David Wray, the leading exponents of the 'Writing Frame' approach, wrote: 'The frames are helpful for children of all ages and abilities from Key Stage 1 to Key Stage 3. However, they are particularly useful for children of average writing ability and those who find writing difficult.'

We acknowledge our debt to the groundbreaking work of Lewis and Wray. However, writing frames are open to abuse and, at worst, can become exercises in sentence completion, as illustrated in Figure 3.

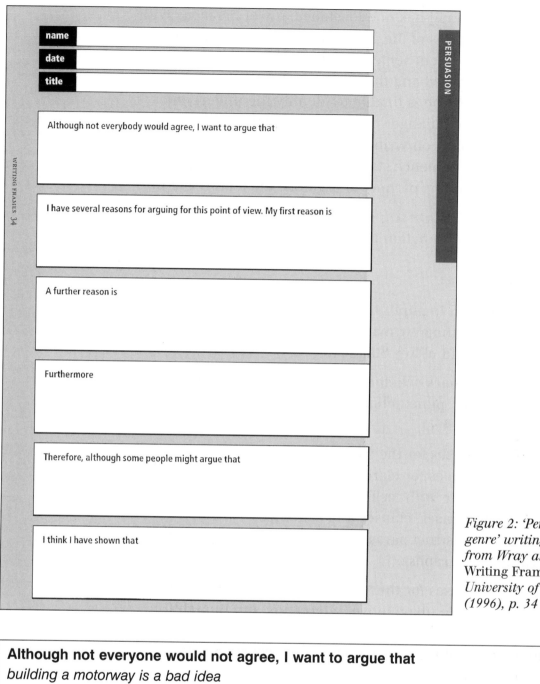

| | |
|---|---|
| **name** | |
| **date** | |
| **title** | |

Although not everybody would agree, I want to argue that

I have several reasons for arguing for this point of view. My first reason is

A further reason is

Furthermore

Therefore, although some people might argue that

I think I have shown that

*Figure 2: 'Persuasion genre' writing frame, from Wray and Lewis, Writing Frames, University of Reading (1996), p. 34*

**Although not everyone would not agree, I want to argue that**
*building a motorway is a bad idea*

**I have several reasons for arguing for this point of view. My first reason is**
*the air will be polluted by fumes*

**A further reason is**
*all the cars will be noisy*

**Furthermore**
*children could be run over*

**Therefore although some people might argue that**
*motorways are a good idea because you can get places fast*

**I think I have shown that**
*we don't want one near our school*

*Figure 3: Completed persuasive writing frame: Year 5 pupil's work in italics*

As can be seen, the pupil has not developed any of his ideas with examples or illustrations of the points he has made. This has been simply an exercise in sentence completion and, if the writing frame is removed and the pupil is asked to discuss or describe the text form, he is unable to identify the underlying structure. The inherent danger of a teaching approach to writing non-fiction based solely on writing frames is that pupils rote-learn a sequence of sentence starters rather than gaining an embedded understanding of how to organise the features of the particular text form.

The two features of non-fiction text forms, namely,
1 Text organisation
2 Language features

are made transparent to pupils through the SUCCESS approach. This clearly links to the new mark scheme employed in the 2003 Writing SAT at the end of Key Stage 2.

For non-fiction the mark scheme is divided into two elements:
1 Sentence structure, punctuation and text organisation
2 Composition and effect

The assessment focuses for the 'Sentence structure' are:
• variation in sentences for clarity, purpose and effect
• (the ability to) write with technical accuracy of syntax and punctuation in phrases, clauses and sentences
• (the ability to) construct paragraphs and use cohesion within and between paragraphs

The assessment focuses for the 'Composition and effect' are:
• (the ability to) write imaginative, interesting and thoughtful texts
• (the ability to) produce texts which are appropriate to tasks, reader and purpose*

The SUCCESS Approach, as outlined in this publication, has been designed to help schools to achieve the higher bands in the new marking system through a consistent whole-school approach designed to enable and empower the pupils as writers in a meaningful way.

*QCA English text mark scheme levels 3-5 (2003)

# The SUCCESS Approach to non-fiction writing

The SUCCESS Approach focuses on making transparent the sequential key features of each non-fiction text form. SUCCESS is our acronym for the various elements of the new approach to the teaching of non-fiction writing outlined in this book:

Structural
Understanding
Confident
Composition
Self Evaluation

=

SUCCESS

## Structural understanding

In the SUCCESS Approach, structural understanding of each non-fiction text form is developed by the following staged teaching sequence designed to improve pupils' acquisition of the text form, rather than merely 'covering' a single literacy objective:

1 Deconstructing an existing example of the text form

2 Teacher modelling of the writing process

3 Using the Success Sheets for drafting and reviewing work.

It is important to note, however, that while the approach underpinning the Success Sheets is relevant throughout the primary school, in Key Stage 1 it should only be undertaken orally and modelled by the teacher. Key Stage 1 pupils should not be asked to complete Success Sheets independently. The only exception might be the use of the Sheets for Writing Instructions with pupils in Year 2 and, even here, we would stress the need for teacher modelling and guidance. Teachers wishing to develop the approach for Writing Recounts, Explanations or Reports (the other forms covered in Year 2) will need to produce their own simplified versions of the Success Sheets which are suitable for their own pupils.

*1 Deconstructing an existing example of the text form*
Deconstructed examples of the text forms can be found in each chapter. Briefly, these consist of:
• a complete example of the text form
• teachers' notes about the structure of the text, with relevant language features and key teaching points.

The examples provided are clearly linked to the structural model presented for each of the text forms, so that the teacher has an example which illustrates the key points relating to structure and language choices as the starting point for the study of the text form. This provides a direct link to Success Sheet 1: Ideas Draft.

Analysing a finished piece of writing is a useful starting point for discussion of the text form. It enables pupils, through talk, to reach an understanding of the text form and its structure before constructing their own written example. In addition to the examples provided, teachers may wish to use their own examples of each text form, such as anonymised pieces by pupils who have already attempted to write in the selected form, either from their own or other schools. QCA and DfES publications and their websites contain many such examples.

*2 Teacher modelling of the writing process*
We recommend that shared writing of the text form, with the teacher acting as scribe, takes place before pupils use the Success Sheets. The purpose of this is that the teacher can discuss the key features of the text form (articulated during the deconstruction activity) and highlight any additional relevant aspects, such as those highlighted in sections 4 and 5 in each chapter.

*3 Using the Success Sheets for drafting and reviewing work*
After deconstruction of an example of the text form and teacher modelling of the writing process, the teacher will introduce Success Sheet 1: Ideas Draft and explain how pupils can use this to plan their writing. It should be stressed that pupils use the column headed 'My own examples' to make notes for their first draft. Many pupils attempt to write the first draft in the boxes provided. In most cases teachers should discourage this practice and insist that pupils write notes because:
• this is better preparation for planning in the long term
• it reinforces note-making skills (see Appendix 1).

Two Success Sheets are provided for each text form. We recommend that teachers increase the size of Success Sheet 1 from A4 to A3 size as this provides more space for pupils to note down their ideas. Sheet 1 supports pupils in the production of their first draft. Sheet 2 helps pupils to look critically at their writing and evaluate it before redrafting. This is achieved by the provision of focused questions which enable them to assess their writing against given criteria for the particular text form, i.e. criteria-based self assessment.

Each Success Sheet is divided into four columns:

*Success Sheet 1: Ideas Draft (example page 12)*

1  The **Features** column consists of sequentially listed elements of the text form – text organisation made transparent! This also provides a standardised language for the text form, so that in discussion of the form a Year 4 teacher would use exactly the same language as the Year 5 or Year 6 teacher. The benefit of such language standardisation in relation to the raising of writing standards is obvious. Currently there is no nationally agreed language to describe the parts of each non-fiction text form.

2  The **Think about!** column makes explicit the language elements required for the successful completion of each text form. The advantage of this approach is that pupils are not guessing how to make their writing effective; the key points are made clear. This makes key assessment criteria clear to the pupil at the preparatory stage of the writing process.

3  The **Examples** column contains a range of sentence starters and modelled examples of effective phrasing. These are directly linked to the 'Think about' column suggestions. A range of sentence starters, as opposed to one given sentence starter, allows pupils to make their own choices, thereby encouraging rather than inhibiting their own styles of writing: making choices is an aspect of active learning. The pupil has to evaluate the alternatives and make a personal choice, thus engaging actively with the writing task. We find this preferable to the more passive completion of a single sentence starter.

4  The **My own examples** column is left blank for pupils to note down their own ideas, using some of the suggestions made in the 'Think about' column as appropriate and making their own selection of language features.

Teachers should be flexible in the way they encourage pupils to use this column. In best practice teachers will encourage their pupils to use this column to make notes, before writing their first draft. However, it is not always necessary for the column to be used in this way; e.g. when writing instructions it will be quite appropriate for the pupil to use this column to write their first draft (as modelled in the 'Examples' column).

## SHEET 1: RECOUNT WRITING (BIOGRAPHY): *Ideas draft*

| Features | Think about! | Example | My own examples |
|---|---|---|---|
| *Title* | Your title should tell the reader who the biography is about in no more than eight words. | The Life of Gandhi | |
| *Overview paragraph* | Your overview paragraph should follow this order:<br>1 Who is it about and what are they best known for?<br>2 When did they live?<br>3 Where did they live?<br>4 Why are they important?<br><br>Answer two or more of the questions in one sentence. | Gandhi (*who*) was a great Indian leader (*main achievement*). He was born in 1869 and died in 1948 (*when*). As a child he lived in West India (*where*), then studied in London, and worked in South Africa, before returning to India at the age of 45 (*when*). He is famous for his peaceful, non violent approach to politics (*why he is important*). | |
| *Childhood events* | Include any childhood events you think are important. | When he was a child Gandhi saw …<br>As a child he … | |
| *Early life, events and achievements* | Tell the reader the important things which happened in the person's early life and perhaps how these influenced his/her later work. | In his early life Gandhi worked as / studied / visited / saw / experienced / thought …… | |
| *Later life , events and achievements* | Tell the reader the important things which happened in the person's later life. Tell the events in the order in which they happened. Indicate whether their later life achievements are more or less important than the earlier ones. | As Gandhi grew older, he …<br>In later life he … | |
| *Concluding paragraph* | Tell the reader the importance or impact of what the person did during his/her life; what we can learn from him/her; how s/he affected others. | Today Gandhi is remembered for …<br>The lesson we can learn …<br>His life is interesting/important because… | |

*Figure 4: Example of Success Sheet 1: Ideas Draft*

*Success Sheet 2: How Well Have I Done? (example page 14)*

1 The **Features** column repeats the language used in Sheet 1, thereby reinforcing the structure of the text form.

2 The **Have I thought about?** column asks the pupil a series of focused questions designed to facilitate criteria-based self assessment of their first draft: a fundamental aspect of the SUCCESS Approach. This is further example of the active learning philosophy which underpins the SUCCESS Approach. By asking pupils to look critically at their own work and decide how to improve it, teachers are enabling them to become independent learners.

3 The **Yes/No** column provides the opportunity for pupils to respond critically to their own work.

4 The column headed **Notes for redrafting** encourages them to make good any omissions in, and to improve the quality of, the initial draft.

### *Confident composition*

The SUCCESS Approach leads to confident composition as it is based on a clear methodology (as outlined already in this introduction) which avoids the danger of handing out photocopied sheets for completion during the lesson.

When Success Sheets are used, the consistency in the language used deepens pupils' understanding of the form, so that genre confusion is eliminated. The combination of standardised features descriptions, criteria-based self-assessment and modelled examples develops pupils' confidence in writing in each form.

The best way to demonstrate the impact of the SUCCESS Approach is through two examples of a Year 5 pupil's work (page 15).

# SHEET 2: RECOUNT WRITING (BIOGRAPHY): *How well have I done?*

| Features | Have I thought about? | Yes/No | Notes for redrafting |
|---|---|---|---|
| *Title* | Does my title tell the reader who my biography is about, in no more than eight words? | | |
| *Overview paragraph* | Does my paragraph follow this order: 1 Who is it about and what is s/he best known for? 2 When did s/he live? 3 Where did s/he live? 4 Why is s/he important? Have I answered two or more of the above in one sentence? | | |
| *Childhood events* | Have I included the important events from his/her childhood? | | |
| *Early life, events and achievements* | Have I told the reader the important things which happened in their early life and how these influenced their later life? | | |
| *Later life, events and achievements* | Have I told the events in the order in which they happened? Have I said which achievements were the most important? | | |
| *Concluding paragraph* | Have I told the reader the importance of what 'X' did during his/her life? Have I told the reader what we can learn from him/her? Or how s/he affected others? | | |

*Figure 5: Example of Success Sheet 2: How well have I done?*

Although not everyone would agree, I want to argue that building a motorway is a bad idea. I have several reasons for arguing for this point of view. My first reason is the air will be polluted by fumes. A further reason is all the cars will be noisy. Furthermore children could be run over. Therefore although some people might argue that motorways are a good idea because you can get places fast. I think I have shown that we don't want one near our school.

*Figure 6: Persuasive writing produced after the use of a writing frame (Year 5 pupil)*

I wish to persuade you that building the motorway on our school grounds will be a terrible idea.

Without a doubt the strongest reason for thinking this is that children like to play and if you build this motorway it will be bad for the children because they won't have any fresh air.

Another reason is one of the children may get run over or injured badly.

Our final reason is you won't be able to get good education because of the sound.

Some parents agree with it because they say they can get to school quick.

To sum up, I think building a motorway is still a despicable idea because people can still get hurt. If this goes ahead the school will be ruined.

*Figure 7: the pupil's first draft after using Success Sheet 1*

## SHEET 2: PERSUASIVE WRITING (level 1): *How well have I done?*

| Features | Have I thought about? | YES/NO | Notes for redrafting |
|---|---|---|---|
| What I think | Is my point of view clearly stated in the first, or first two, sentences? | Yes | |
| | Have I written in the first person 'I'? | Yes | |
| First reason for thinking this | Have I used my strongest argument first? | Not sure | |
| | Is it expressed in one or two sentences? | Yes | Children could get asthma if they don't get fresh air. |
| | Have I expanded my strongest argument by adding details or examples? | not really | |
| | Have I used questions to involve the reader's emotions? | No | How would you feel if your child had to breathe in bad air? |
| Second reason for thinking this | Have I started a new paragraph for my next strongest argument? | No | If a lorry crashed lots of children could be killed not just one. |
| | Have I expanded my argument by giving examples or details? | No | This is the strongest, put it in the first reason bit. |
| | Have I used a variety of linking words or phrases to connect my ideas? | Yes | |
| Third reason for thinking this | Have I started another new paragraph for the argument which is third in importance? | Yes | |
| | Have I remembered examples/details? | No | You couldn't concentrate on your lessons because of the noise like ambulances or police cars. |
| | Have I varied my choice of linking words or phrases? | Yes | |
| Reasons why other people think differently | Have I started a new paragraph? | Yes | |
| | Have I explained why other people might think differently / hold a different point of view? | Yes | Parents – change quick to get to school faster than they can now |
| Summary of what I think | Have I summarised the main reasons for my point of view – no details or examples this time? | Yes | |
| | Have I repeated my strongest argument using different words this time? | No | I will change my first one because getting hurt is stronger than fresh air. |
| | Have I used appropriate words to show this is my final paragraph? | Yes | |

*Figure 8: a copy of the pupil's completed Success Sheet 2 – self-assessment/preparation for redrafting.*

> I wish to persuade you that building the motorway on our school grounds will be a terrible idea.
>
> Without a doubt the strongest reason for thinking this is people can get hurt. Children could get run over or injured badly if we have a motorway. If a lorry crashed lots of children could be killed not just one.
>
> Another reason for thinking this is that children like to play and if you build this motorway it will be bad for the children because they won't have any fresh air. Children could get asthma if they don't get fresh air. How would you feel if your child had to breathe in bad air?
>
> Our final reason is you won't be able to get good education because of the sound. You couldn't concentrate on your lessons because of the noise like ambulances or police cars.
>
> Some parents agree with it because they say they can get to school faster than they can now.
>
> To sum up, I think building a motorway is still a despicable idea because people can still get hurt. If this goes ahead the school will be ruined.

*Figure 9: the pupil's redrafted persuasive writing*

In the first example (Figure 6), note that there is no difference between the text which was filled in on the writing frame and the final piece of writing. The second example (Figure 7) is the pupil's first draft after using Success Sheet 1. Using Success Sheet 1 has enabled the pupil to paragraph his work successfully. In Figure 8, observe how the pupil's self-assessment has led to his inclusion of examples and the re-ordering of points in the final version. Figure 9, the redrafted text, is a more developed piece of writing, providing illustrations and examples to flesh out the main points the pupil wished to make.

## *Evaluation*

'Success Sheet 2: How well have I done?' is a tool to enable pupils to look critically at their own work and evaluate it against given criteria for each text form. This can then be used to redraft and improve work, as can be seen in Figures 7–9. However, there are occasions when the evaluation and suggestions for improvement can be viewed as an end in themselves. It may not always be necessary for pupils to write a redrafted version of the text if their intentions for improvement are clear and their judgements are sound.

In the recommended sequence of lessons (which may be found in section 7, Teachers' Notes) we suggest that once pupils have completed an evaluation of their work and indicated their intentions for improving it, or after they have written a redrafted version, the teacher then provides the pupil with feedback about their evaluation of their work. In developing pupils' skills of self-assessment, it is essential that the teacher validates the pupils evaluation or indicates where their evaluation is not accurate, where it is too harsh or too lenient in the way the criteria have been applied. This dialogue will deepen pupils' understanding of the criteria and also provide them with a growing understanding of standards. Criteria can be met to different standards and it is important that pupils understand what is expected of them.

The ability to review, evaluate and self-assess requires higher order skills which require direct teaching. Thus the use of Success Sheet 2 and the way it can be used to develop these skills is integral to the approach we are taking. By teaching structural understanding, enabling confident composition and developing self-assessment skills, we shall enable pupils to be independent writers and raise the quality of their work.

### *The benefits of the SUCCESS Approach*

If the Success Sheets included in this book are used in the manner we describe, then, by the end of Key Stage 2, most pupils should be able to verbally describe the key features (and the elements that make up these features) of each non-fiction text form. Pupils who are able to do this will have internalised the structure of each text form, thus freeing up valuable thinking space which can be used to concentrate on improving the quality of their work, by focusing on its content and the effective use of language.

All the support sheets can be used successfully without adaptation in most situations. However, teachers are in the best position to know how to meet the different individual needs of their pupils in relation to the demands of a specific writing task. Consequently they may wish to alter or adapt the Success Sheets in order to ensure that the readability level is appropriate for their pupils. We do not, however, recommend altering the 'Features' column. The rationale for this is simple; if the language used to describe the features of each text form is common throughout the school, then pupils' assimilation of the form will become embedded.

In Chapter 4, 'Writing reports' and Chapter 6, 'Persuasive writing', teachers can see examples of how the basic support sheets have been adapted for different purposes.

In conclusion, teachers may wish to make adaptations in relation to:
• the need for differentiation for groups, or individuals, in a class;

- NLS Framework objectives for the same text form in different year groups;
- the subject being taught (cross-curricular teaching of non-fiction forms is of prime importance as it provides real contexts for writing – see Chapter 4).

This book encompasses all of the non-fiction text forms which pupils are expected to cover in the primary school. Each chapter is dedicated to a single non-fiction text form: instructions, recounts, explanations, reports, newspaper reports, persuasion and discussion.

Each chapter follows a similar layout for ease of use:
1 Definition of text form
2 National Literacy Strategy links
3 Text level features (purpose and organisation)
4 Sentence level features (style, punctuation, grammar)
5 Word level features (vocabulary, spelling)
6 Note-making related to the text form
7 Teachers' notes, which contains a recommended sequence of lessons
8 Activity suggestions
9 Writing Success Sheets

The critical tests for the success of any teaching methods are:
- Can the pupil remember and use the skills and approaches at a later date?
- Does the pupil have the capacity to transfer, or generalise, what they have been taught to related, but not entirely similar, tasks?

Improving the capacity to transfer is achieved by developing pupils' skills in self monitoring. If pupils have a clear purpose for writing and the Success Sheets are used in the manner outlined (with an accent on pupil enjoyment and excitement !) then their work will undoubtedly improve, ultimately leading to effectively structured non-fiction writing. We have written this book in order to enable pupils to become more confident, independent writers capable of making informed decisions about their own writing.

# 1  Writing instructions

## 1  Definition

When writing instructions, the writer spells out for the reader what is needed, and the stages to be gone through, in order to carry out a task successfully. Instructions are a relatively simple form of non-fiction writing. Pupils become familiar with instructions early on when playing games, learning to use equipment, making artefacts, cooking and so on. As instructions are usually written in simple sentences, using straightforward, direct language, most pupils can write instructions for a simple task by the time they complete Key Stage 1.

## 2  NLS Framework links

### Year 1 Term 1

* **T16** 'to write and draw simple instructions for everyday classroom use'

### Year 2 Term 1

* **T15** 'to write simple instructions, e.g. getting to school, playing a game'
* **T16** 'to use models from reading to organise instructions sequentially, e.g. listing points in order, each point depending on the previous one, numbering'
* **T17** 'to use diagrams in instructions, e.g. drawing and labelling diagrams as part of a set of instructions'
* **T18** ' to use appropriate register in writing instructions, i.e. direct, impersonal, building on texts read'

### Year 3 Term 2

* **T16** 'to write instructions e.g. rules for games, recipes, using a range of organisational devices, e.g. lists, dashes, commas for lists in sentences, recognising the importance of correct sequence; use 'writing frames' as appropriate for support'

### Year 4 Term 1

* **T25** 'to write clear instructions using conventions learned from reading'
* **T26** 'to improve the cohesion of written instructions and directions through the use of link phrases and organisational devices such as subheadings and numbering'

### Year 5 Term 1

* **T25** 'to write instructional texts, and test them out, e.g. instructions for loading computers, design briefs for technology, rules for games'

## 3 Text level features (purpose and organisation)

*Organisation*

Instructions may be organised as follows:
- title
- requirements/ingredients (what is needed)
- method (how to make/play/carry out the task)
- concluding paragraph (how success can be measured)

## 4 Sentence level features (style, punctuation and grammar)

*Style*
- use of bullet points/alpha-ordering/numbering
- new lines for each step of the method
- use of diagrams and annotated sketches to augment text
- short precise sentences
- layout and use of space (see teachers' notes)
- use of techniques for emphasising key words – e.g. emboldening, increasing font size, block capitals

*Punctuation*
- use of commas to separate items in lists

*Grammar*
- consistent use of the imperative/command language

## 5 Word level features (vocabulary, spelling)

*Vocabulary*
- use of simple, direct vocabulary
- use of sequential connectives – e.g. *first, next, then*
- use of action verbs – e.g. *take, place*
- use of adverbs of manner to increase the precision of instructions – e.g. *slowly, carefully, gently*

*Spelling*
- *First, next, then, after that*
- *Firstly, secondly* etc.
- Subject-specific words

## 6 Writing instructions and note making

As indicated above, when pupils are writing instructions many of the techniques of effective note-making are used:
- using space to clarify different steps
- enumeration or alpha ordering
- use of headings and subheadings
- use of annotated diagrams or patterns

As instructions are written sequentially, the note-making pattern most useful for organising ideas is the flow chart, which can be taught and reinforced on each occasion when pupils are required to write instructions, e.g.

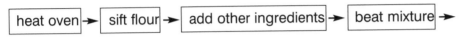

## 7 Teachers' notes

When teaching the writing of instructions we recommend that, whenever possible, the writing activity should be linked to hands-on experiences, such as writing recipes when a cooking activity is being undertaken.

There are many occasions across the curriculum where the activity can provide an opportunity to write instructions, e.g.
- designing and making artefacts in Design and Technology
- playing a game in PE
- outlining procedures for specific classroom activities
- procedures for carrying out a science investigation
- procedures for operating the computer or using a particular computer program.

If the teacher maximises experiential learning opportunities, the pupils are more likely to gain an embedded understanding of the writing form.

When working with older pupils who have already written instructions based on direct experience, teachers may wish to consider augmenting experiential approaches by providing them with opportunities to write instructions as part of a fictional task, such as writing the instructions for Jack to plant his magic beans.

The layout of instructions is very important as it must assist the reader to follow the sequence of steps to be taken. Leaving space between the different steps helps to provide even greater clarity for the reader. Teachers will wish to stress these key points.

When we look at the requirements for writing instructions as outlined in the NLS Framework, we can see that as pupils become more proficient, what changes is, usually, the complexity of the task for which instructions have to be provided, along with a move from the use of simple vocabulary and sentence structures to more technical and precise vocabulary and complex sentence structures. At this point teachers will wish to emphasise further organisational devices such as the use of headings, subheadings, numbering and link phrases. Pupils should be encouraged to use techniques for highlighting key points or keywords such as underlining, emboldening, increasing font size and use of block capitals.

The following language sequences are often taught to help pupils to organise their instructions.

1 Single word starters
- *First ...*
- *Next ...*
- *Then ...*
- *After that ...*
- *Last of all ...*

Words such as *repeat, continue*

2 Enumeration
- *Firstly ...*
- *Secondly ...*
- *Thirdly ...*
- NB Pupils have to be explicitly told *not* to continue this sequence as *Fourthly, Fifthly*. For this reason, we suggest that pupils are encouraged to use numbering or alpha ordering as alternatives to enumeration.

The introduction of more complex language sequences needs to be handled with care as this can result in pupils using words incorrectly or inappropriately, as this example from a Year 2 pupil illustrates:

---

Instructions for making the Lighthousekeeper's Lunch

- First take a slice of bread.
- Second spread butter on it.
- Next add ham, lettuce and tomato.
- Then put another slice of bread on top.
- Penultimately cut the sandwich in two.
- Finally eat the sandwich.

---

Clearly the use of complex connectives in the last two steps is inappropriate in the context of this task. The complexity of the language used is directly linked to the nature of the instructional task.

*Recommended sequence of lessons*

1 Deconstruction of existing instructions, chosen to match the writing objectives for the year group (see Activity 1).

2 An optional additional activity which would be appropriate for Year 3 pupils is suggested in Activity 2: sequencing instructions. This would support the NLF objective 'to recognise the importance of correct sequencing'.

3 Modelling of required text during a shared writing session, focusing on the key points brought out in the deconstruction activity (see suggestions for instructional writing tasks in the teachers' notes on page 22).

4 Pupils make notes for their own instructions using Success Sheet 1.

5 Pupils write their own instructions.

6 Pupils evaluate their instructions using Success Sheet 2.

7 An appropriate activity for Year 5 pupils who have written instructions is suggested in Activity 3: testing instructions. This would support the NLF objective 'to write instructional texts and test them out'.

8 Teacher provides feedback to pupils on their instructions and evaluations – this can be done orally or in writing, as appropriate to the age/stage of development of their pupils.

9 Teacher summarises what has been learned with class.

## 8 Activity suggestions

*Activity 1: Deconstructing instructions*

We suggest that deconstructing an existing example is the best starting point for any sequence of lessons aimed at developing pupils' writing skills in a particular genre or form. Teachers can use the example provided (Figure 1.1, page 26) as a vehicle for identifying the key features of instructional writing (at text, sentence and word level) with their class or group.

However, teachers will wish to adapt the approach modelled here to the aspect of instruction writing they are working on with their class, e.g. deconstructing an example of illustrated instructions as a starting point with Year 1 pupils, annotated diagrams with Year 2 pupils and so on.

*Activity 2: Sequencing instructions*

Pupils working in pairs are given an envelope of cards containing the instructions for carrying out a task. Each card contains only one stage of the instructions. Pupils have to work out the correct sequence and place the cards in the correct order for carrying out the task. This can be differentiated by having tasks ranging from those with relatively few steps (for younger or less able pupils) to more complex tasks with a greater number of steps for older or more able pupils. The sequencing task can be devised in such a way that pupils are asked to identify the language sequence which enabled them to organise the instructions for the task.

On page 28 there is a set of instructions for making a bangle (as part of a D&T exercise) which may be used for this activity.

*Activity 3: Testing instructions*

A good way of testing the accuracy of instructions is to ask a group of pupils not involved in writing instructions ('the testing group') to follow instructions written previously by a different group of pupils ('the writing group'). The accuracy of the instructions will be gauged by whether or not they can be followed to a successful outcome. If the outcome is not successful, 'the testing group' can highlight for the original writing group which steps need to be redrafted. (This can be carried out by pairs or individuals as well as groups.) The initial instruction writing task can be differentiated by providing a range of tasks for groups of differing ability – simpler tasks for less able groups of pupils, more complex tasks for more able. Teachers will also need to differentiate the 'testing task' to enable all 'testing groups' to provide meaningful feedback to the 'writing group'.

*Activity 4: Fictionalised instructions*

To undertake this activity teachers may base an instructional writing task on a fiction text. The following texts are suggested as possible choices:

| | |
|---|---|
| *The Borrowers* by Mary Norton | ➤ How to shrink to the size of a pea |
| *The BFG* by Roald Dahl | ➤ Instructions for making the giant's breakfast |
| *Beowolf* (Ian Serraillier's version) | ➤ Instructions for getting to Grendel's lair |
| *Harry Potter and the Philosopher's Stone* by J K Rowling | ➤ Instructions for playing Quidditch |

**SHEET 1 : INSTRUCTIONAL WRITING**
**IDEAS DRAFT**

| Features | Think about ! | Examples | My own examples |
|---|---|---|---|
| **Title** | Tell the reader what is to be made or done in no more than seven words | <u>How to</u> bake a cake <br> <u>How to</u> play Scrabble <br> <u>How to</u> get to Paris by train | How to make a cup of tea . |
| **Requirements / Ingredients** (What is needed) | List what will be needed to make / play or do it <br> Consider using one of the following : <br> 1 } <br> 2 } numbering <br> 3 } <br> OR <br> a } <br> b } alpha-ordering <br> c } <br> OR <br> • } <br> • } bullet points <br> • } <br> Don't forget to start a new line for each new item | You will need : <br> 1   Three eggs <br> 2   Two level tablespoons of sugar <br> 3   150 grams of flour…..etc <br> OR <br> a   Two or more players <br> b   A Scrabble board <br> c   Letter tiles …..etc <br> OR <br> •   A copy of the London to Paris timetable <br> •   A valid rail ticket <br> •   A railcard, if you have one | You will need: <br> • Cup/Mug <br> • Kettle <br> • Tea pot <br> • Tea leaves/Tea bags <br> • Sugar (optional) <br> • Milk or A slice of Lemon <br> • A teaspoon <br> • Water |
| **Method** (How to make / play / do it) | Don't forget to start a new paragraph when you begin the method. <br> Tell the reader how to make / play / do it. <br> Don't forget to list the steps in order | First….. <br> Next….. <br> Then….. <br> After that …..etc <br> OR <br> Firstly….. <br> Secondly…..etc <br> OR <br> Primarily….. <br> Furthermore….. <br> Moreover…..etc | Firstly, put the water into the kettle and switch on to boil. <br> Next, put the tea leaves/bags in the teapot and fill with boiling water then leave it to stand. <br> Then, pour tea into cup/mug and add milk/lemon/sugar as required |
| **Concluding paragraph** (How the reader knows s/he has been successful) | Tell the reader how they will know they have been successful | When it is finished it will…. <br> You will now be able to….. <br> Now that you have…..you can….. | When it is finished, stir as necessary, and drink preferably with biscuits. |

*Figure 1.1 How to make a cup of tea: completed Success Sheet 1, pupil at Stalyhill County Junior School, Tameside*

*Title* # Instructions for completing your holiday topic

*Requirements* You will need:

- to decide which country you will write about

- books, magazine articles about the country

*Method*
- First choose the country you would like to holiday in.

- Next make a list of the things you want to find out about that country.

- Then list the books and pamphlets we have in the classroom which you might use during your topic.

- After that check all the books and pamphlets to see which are likely to be useful (look at the titles, contents and index and quickly skim through).

- Then plan your topic into sections, each one describing a different aspect of your country.

- After that read the books and pamphlets and make notes as you read. Use the different aspects you want to find out about as the headings for your notes.

- Check with your original list to see that you've found out all the things you wanted to know.

  Finally write up your findings in your own words, in a booklet, remembering to include:
  1 Title page
  2 Contents
  3 Bibliography
  4 Index

*Concluding paragraph* Now that you have completed your booklet add it to the library display of holiday booklets.

# Instructions for making a bangle

You will need:

• coloured wool

• a selection of coloured beads

• a few gold and/or silver beads

• First choose the colour of wool you want for your bangle.

• Now cut off the length of wool you need. Remember to make it long enough to go round your wrist and tie a bow.

• Knot your wool at one end so that the beads won't fall off.

• After that choose the coloured beads you want and 4 or 5 silver or gold beads.

• Decide if you are going to make a pattern with the beads.

• Then thread your beads on to the wool following your pattern if you are having one.

• While you are threading, spread the gold or silver beads out as evenly as you can.

• Continue threading beads until there are enough on the wool to go completely round your wrist (or the wrist of the person you are making it for).

• Last of all knot the other end of the thread and tie a bow.

• You now have a bangle you can wear or give to a friend.

# SUCCESS SHEET 1: WRITING INSTRUCTIONS: *Ideas draft*

| Features | Think about! | Example | My own examples |
|---|---|---|---|
| *Title* | Tell the reader what is to be done in no more than seven words. | How to bake a cake | |
| *Requirements/ Ingredients (What is needed)* | List what will be needed to carry out the task.<br><br>Consider using:<br>numbering (1, 2 …)<br>alpha-ordering (a, b, c ….)<br>bullet points.<br><br>Don't forget to start a new line for each new item. | You will need:<br>1. 3 large eggs<br>2. 175 grams sugar<br>3. 175 grams soft margarine<br>4. 200 grams flour<br>5. 3 tablespoons of milk<br><br>You will also need a cake tin greased and lined with greaseproof paper. | |
| *Method (how to make/ play/do it)* | Tell the reader how to make/play/ do it.<br><br>List the steps in order.<br><br>Don't forget to start a new line for each new instruction. | First … pre-heat the oven to 170 C.<br><br>Next … sift the flour into a bowl.<br><br>Then … add the other ingredients.<br><br>and stir with a wooden spoon.<br><br>Beat … the mixture for 1 minute.<br><br>After that … spoon the mixture …<br><br>Finally … bake in the oven … | |
| *Concluding paragraph* | Tell the reader how they will know they have been successful | When it is finished it will …<br><br>You will now be able to …<br><br>Now that you have … you can … | |

# SUCCESS SHEET 2: WRITING INSTRUCTIONS: *How well have I done?*

| Features | Have I thought about? | YES/NO | Notes for redrafting |
|---|---|---|---|
| *Title* | Does my title tell the reader what is being made or done in no more than seven words? | | |
| *Requirements/ Ingredients (What is needed)* | Have I listed what is needed?<br><br>Did I consider using one of the following:<br>   numbering<br>   alpha-ordering<br>   bullet points ?<br><br>Have I remembered to start a new line for each new item? | | |
| *Method (how to make/ play do it)* | Have I remembered to start a new line?<br><br>Do my instructions tell the reader how to make/ play/do it?<br><br>Have I remembered to list my steps in order? | | |
| *Concluding paragraph* | Have I told the reader how they will know they've been successful? | | |

30

# 2 Writing recounts

## 1 Definition

When writing recounts, the writer retells past experiences to inform or entertain the reader. Recounts can be written for different audiences, which may be known or unknown to the writer. The audience will influence the tone of the recount and this can affect both the style and the formality of the language used. Pupils should be provided with opportunities to write for both known and unknown readers – e.g. writing an account of a day out to entertain a friend, of a school trip to inform classmates in another class, of the Fire of London or the life of Florence Nightingale to inform unknown readers. A key feature of recounts is the sequential organisation of information.

## 2 NLS Framework links

### Year 1 Term 3
- **T20** 'to write simple recounts linked to topics of interest/study or to personal experience, using the language of texts read as models for own writing. Make group/class books, e.g. our day at school, our trip to ...'

### Year 2 Term 3
- **T16** 'to write non-fiction texts, using texts read as models for own writing'

### Year 3 Term 3
- **T22** 'experiment with recounting the same event in a variety of ways, e.g. in the form of a letter'

### Year 5 Term 1
- **T24** ' to write recounts based on subject, topic or personal experiences for (a) a close friend and (b) an unknown reader, e.g. an account of a field trip, a match, a historical event'

### Year 6 Term 1
- **T14** 'to develop the skills of biographical and autobiographical writing in role'

## 3 Text level features (purpose and organisation)

*Organisation*
At its most simple, the organisation of recounts involves:
- title
- overview or orientation paragraph
- events organised sequentially
- concluding paragraph

## 4  Sentence level features (style, punctuation and grammar)

*Style*
- use of a condensed synopsis of the whole at the beginning
- use of language appropriate for time sequencing to link paragraphs
- use of summarising or evaluative final paragraph
- choice of tone and language appropriate to the audience selected

*Punctuation*
- use of paragraphing to separate events
- correct use of commas within sentences to mark phrases or clauses

*Grammar*
- consistent use of the past tense
- consistent use of the first person when based on personal experience
- consistent use of third person when recount is biographical or historical or something that happened to a friend

## 5  Word level features (vocabulary, spelling)

*Vocabulary*
- use of broad range of temporal connectives as appropriate for the intended audience – e.g. *first, next, then, before, prior to, after that, as well as, in the future*

*Spelling*
- words specific to the subject or events being recounted
- *yesterday, today*
- *before, after that, next*
- *prior to, furthermore, moreover*

## 6  Note-making and writing recounts

As recounts are written chronologically, an important aspect of note-making to be covered when dealing with this text form is a timeline (see Activity 2).

When recording their own ideas or information gathered when carrying out research, we have found that pupils often find it difficult to write in note form. For this reason it is important that, from a very early stage, teachers stress the difference between making notes and writing a first draft, and model the process of recording keywords and phrases. Pupils should be instructed to use key words and phrases only when making notes and not complete sentences.

## 7 Teachers' notes

Recount writing is regarded by many teachers as the simplest form of non-fiction writing, since recounts are organised chronologically. Recounts are often seen by pupils, particularly in the earlier stages of developing this form, as writing a 'true story'.

There are many opportunities for examining and writing recounts across the curriculum, e.g.:
- in geography or history, recounting what happened on a field trip or visit
- recounting historical events
- in history, art and music there are opportunities to write biographical recounts.

*Recounts of trips and visits*

A common choice, and a good starting point, for writing recounts is to focus on events or activities in which individual pupils and/or groups have taken part, such as a school trip or visit. In such cases teachers should stress the use of the first person (*I/we*) and the fact that recounts of this type are generally written in the past tense.

After deconstructing an existing recount as the first step in introducing pupils to this form, teachers could use a class or school trip to model the writing task with their pupils. When modelling this form teachers will wish to use 'talk aloud' methods to accentuate the importance of maintaining chronological order and the use of temporal connectives. The teacher will also wish to stress the need to vary the choice of connectives, e.g. 'I've used *After that* to begin the last paragraph, so I'd better begin the next one with *Then we*.'

The best recounts contain an overview paragraph to orientate the reader to the subject of the account. We think it is important to stress the need to be concise when writing this paragraph. If the paragraph contains too much detail, then it is clearly not an overview. In order to ensure that pupils are concise, we suggest that teachers encourage pupils to write the overview paragraph in no more than four sentences. As this is one less sentence than the number of questions the pupils are asked to consider in our suggested model, pupils are thus compelled to combine sentences to produce complex and/or compound sentences.

*Recounts based on research: historical events and biographies*

Most of the text organisation features of the 'Trips and Visits' recounts and of historical or biographical recounts are similar. Two essential differences, however, need to be highlighted.

- Biographies and historical recounts are written in the third person
- The depth of the research carried out by the pupil will determine the quality of the final piece of writing.

Since both recount forms involving research are tackled in Years 5 and 6, research skills will have been taught at an earlier stage. It is important that pupils have learned to handle information from a range of resources before undertaking the writing of a recount based on research – information from books, the internet, databases, photographic and original sources (such as letters or eyewitness accounts). The way resources are managed is one way in which the teacher can differentiate the research aspect of a recount writing activity, for example by providing different resources for different ability groups, or creating mixed ability groups where all information gathered is shared with all members of the group. Teacher modelling of how to interrogate resources and handle the information gathered (including taking notes, organising the information chronologically, and modelling the process of transforming notes back into prose text) is an essential part of teaching pupils how to carry out independent research. (See Appendix 1, page 169.)

*Historical events*

Teachers may wish to use information which has been gathered during work on a particular historical topic as the basis for a recount writing task. The key features of text organisation are similar to trips and visits, with the focus on writing events in a sequential order, using the past tense. Historical recounts are generally written in the third person, except when the teacher might choose to make the recount an eyewitness account, in which case this would be an occasion when it would be appropriate to use first person recounting. The other major difference when writing a recount of historical events is the inclusion of cause and effect. In most cases teachers will want to encourage their pupils to explain the result or outcome of the events they are recounting.

*Biographies*

Another type of recount which requires research is the biography: an account of a person's life written by a pupil or pupils.

When research into a person's life has been completed, and before writing the draft biography, the teacher may wish to explore the meaning of the word 'impact' as used in Success Sheet 1, column 2, concluding paragraph. We think the following definition of impact may be helpful to pupils
- *impact* = the difference his/her life made
- *impact* = the effect of his/her life on others

This is an aspect which pupils in Year 6 should consider when writing a biography of a famous person.

With regard to the NLF objective Year 6 Term 1 T14 'to develop the skills of biographical and autobiographical writing in role', teachers may wish to interpret this both in terms of asking pupils to write their own autobiographies, but also to imagine themselves in the position of another person (e.g. a child worker in the mines in the 19th century or an evacuee during the Second World War) and write this person's autobiography. This is an occasion when it would be appropriate to write in the first person. This kind of empathic writing can demonstrate the pupils' understanding of the historical context and provide a general view of the lives of such people. In using the Success Sheets relating to biography, it will, therefore, be important that teachers edit them appropriately to match the type of biography they intend their pupils to write.

*Using the Success Sheets*

Three versions of the Success Sheets are provided at the end of this chapter, one set for trips and visits, one for historical recounts and one for biographies. There are minor differences between the versions in order to match them to the required form of recount. Teachers should select (and adapt if necessary) the ones most appropriate for the writing task they have chosen.

*Recommended sequence of lessons*

1 Deconstruction of an existing recount, to match the writing objectives for the year group (see Activity 1).
2 Teacher models how to make notes for the recount by creating a timeline (see Activity 2).
3 Pupils make notes for their recount using the timeline approach, either individually or in pairs or small groups.

4 Shared writing session, demonstrating how to organise the notes (following the model outlined in Success Sheet 1) and focussing on key points highlighted during the deconstruction activity.

5 Using the model demonstrated by the teacher, pupils plan their own recount using the appropriate version of Success Sheet 1 and write their first draft.

6 Pupils evaluate their recount using the appropriate Success Sheet 2.

7 Teacher provides feedback to pupils on their recounts and evaluations – this can be done orally or in writing, as appropriate to the age/stage of development of their pupils.

8 Teacher summarises what has been learned about this text form with the class.

It should be noted that the Success Sheets have been designed for the recount text form. Year 3 and Year 5 NLF objectives require pupils to recount an event in a variety of ways and for different audiences. In such cases, it may not be appropriate to use the Success Sheets provided in this chapter.

## 8  Activity suggestions

*Activity 1: Deconstruction of existing recount*

Teachers can use the example provided (page 38) as a vehicle for discussion of the key features of this text form. We suggest that deconstructing an existing example is the best starting point for any sequence of lessons aimed at developing pupils' writing skills in a particular genre or form. Teachers can use the example as a vehicle for identifying the key features of  writing a recount (at text, sentence and word level) with their class or group.

The example given was written by an upper Key Stage 2 pupil to inform pupils in a parallel class about their trip to Oldham Museum.

*Activity 2: Timelines (1)*

In creating a timeline, it is a good idea to get pupils to record the events which they are to recount on separate cards and, once all the notes have been made, to organise their cards into a timeline. This approach will work for recounting outings or trips, personal accounts, events from history and any form of biographical writing. There are many advantages to this approach:

• it enables pupils who gather the information haphazardly to organise it sequentially

- pupils gain an overview of events before they begin to plan their writing
- from the overview they are able to establish the relative importance of different events and reflect this in their written recount
- the timeline can be used to check that all relevant information has been included in their recount.

*Activity 3: Timelines (2)*

Teachers may prefer to carry out this activity before Timelines (1) in order to give their pupils practice in making a timeline.

We have created an obituary for an imaginary MP, Gordon Butler (page 39). From this obituary, pupils can create a timeline for his life. The first and last events on the timeline are:
- Born 16 August 1912 in Glasgow
- Died 9 January 2003 at his home in Glasgow.

*Activity 4: Writing for different audiences*

NLF objective Year 5 Term 1 T24 is 'to write recounts based on subject, topic or personal experiences for (a) a close friend and (b) an unknown reader, e.g. an account of a field trip, a match, a historical event'.

To meet this objective teachers might use an existing recount which pupils have written (e.g. of a school event) and ask them to use the information and adapt it into (a) a letter to a friend, then (b) an account to be included in a handout to parents about the school. Shared writing of the opening paragraph of each version would allow issues related to formality/informality of language to be discussed before the pupils complete the writing tasks.

Alternatively, teachers might choose to take an existing recount of a historical event written for an unknown reader, and ask pupils to imagine they had been there and were recounting the event either for a friend or as a newscaster reporting the event as it happened, or as a reporter for a newspaper ('VE Day', page 40 could be used for this task, if the class were studying the Second World War).

Newspaper reports are generally recounts of events, adapted for the newspaper's readership and presented in the form required. (See Chapter 5: Writing newspaper reports)

| | | |
|---|---|---|
| **Title** | **Our trip to Oldham Museum** | *Note:* |
| **Overview paragraph** | Yesterday our class, with Mrs Jones, went to Oldham Museum. We went to find out more about what life was like in Victorian times, by visiting the Victoria Street downstairs and looking at some of their objects. | – *the coverage of:*<br>• *Who*<br>• *When*<br>• *Where* |
| **Event 1** | Before we went we made our classroom into a Victorian one by putting all the desks in rows. Mrs Jones carried a big stick called a cane! We also read a book in Literacy about a Victorian chimney sweep. They even had to work at weekends. | – *preparation for the trip*<br><br>– *the use of 'Before we went ...' and 'We also ...'* |
| **Event 2** | When we arrived we walked down the stairs to the Victorian street. We found out they had gas lights not electric and we looked in the cobbler's window. They had clogs not shoes like we do. I liked it when we went in the Victorian pub. It had a bowl for spitting in. | – *the interesting things that happened when they arrived*<br><br>– *the use of 'When we arrived..'* |
| **Next events** | After that we visited the education room. We saw a black dress that women wore if their husband died. It is called a mourning dress.<br><br>In addition we held the doll with the wax head. You couldn't put it near a fire or it would melt. | – *the use of 'After that..'*<br><br><br>– *the use of 'In addition..'* |
| **Concluding paragraph** | The most interesting thing was the Victorian pub. I have never been in a pub before and it was good to see what they were like a long time ago. | – *evaluative ending* |

# Obituary: Gordon Butler

Gordon Butler, who has died aged 90, was a working class Labour MP whose love of libraries as an instrument of universal education left a strong mark on the House of Commons and on his native city of Glasgow.

He was born on 16 May 1912 in Springburn Road, Glasgow. Always a bright child at school, he won a scholarship to St Patrick's Academy in 1923.

When he was 14, however, his father died and he had no option but to leave school and follow in his father's footsteps, taking a job in the railway workshop at Cowlairs. This was the time when the Springburn area of Glasgow built steam engines for the world.

He served his time as a toolmaker and by the early 1930s was active in the National Union of Railwaymen. He never gave up his interest in education and became a tutor for the National Council of Labour Colleges.

In 1936 he married Jane Brown in St Patrick's Cathedral. Together they had eight children.

He joined the Labour Party in 1938. During the war his occupation was reserved and after the war he was elected to Glasgow City Council. He was a gifted speaker and became one of the most powerful men on the council, eventually holding office as the city treasurer.

Following the death of his wife in 1963, he stood for Parliament and became an MP in 1964.

He remained interested in education, seeing it as the key to the country's prosperity. His valuable work within the Labour Party led to his appointment as Parliamentary Private Secretary to successive Treasury ministers from 1967-70.

He became chairman of the committee managing the library of the House of Commons, a role he enjoyed until his retirement from politics.

He eventually retired from politics in 1979, preferring to spend his time back in his native city.

He continued to serve on a wide range of bodies, all connected with education in some way. He was a member of the Scottish Examinations Council from 1981-85 and President of the Scottish Libraries Association from 1985-90.

He will be long remembered for his contributions to the City of Glasgow and the Scottish political scene.

He is survived by his second wife, Mary, whom he married in 1975, six of his eight children and seven grandchildren.

John Black, MP for Rutherglen

*Gordon Butler, politician, born August 16 1912; died January 9 2003.*

# VE Day

In Britain, it was announced that the following day, May 8th, would be 'VE Day', a national holiday to celebrate the victory. Everywhere, people hung out banners and Union Jacks. They sang, danced, cheered, let off fireworks and built bonfires to burn guys that were dressed up to look like Hitler. People brought out tables and chairs and there were street parties to celebrate the end of the war. Churchill broadcast a special message on the radio, and large crowds gathered to cheer him outside the House of Commons. He made several public appearances, waving to the crowd and giving his 'V for Victory' sign. When night fell, all the lights, including the searchlights, were turned on, so that the cities looked as bright as possible.

'VE Day', from *Daily Life in a Wartime House*

# SUCCESS SHEET 1: RECOUNT WRITING (NON-FICTION: TRIPS AND VISITS): *Ideas draft*

| Features | Think about! | Example | My own examples |
|---|---|---|---|
| *Title* | Your title should tell the reader what the recount is about in no more than eight words. | My/Our Trip to the Castle | |
| *Overview paragraph* | Write your overview paragraph in the past tense.<br>It should tell the reader<br>• When the trip happened.<br>• Who was involved.<br>• Where it happened.<br>• Why it happened.<br>• What you did.<br><br>Answer two or more of the above in one sentence. | Last Tuesday (*when*) our class (*who*) went on a bus (*how*) trip to the castle (*where*) to learn about what life was like in the olden days (*why*). We were shown lots of interesting things and then we made a plan of the castle (*what*). | |
| *Event 1* | Tell the reader about any planning or preparation you did, e.g. reading books, searching the internet.<br><br>Think about what will really interest the reader. Will it really be the journey? Or what you ate? | Prior to our trip, we …<br><br>Before we went … | |
| *Event 2* | Tell the reader the first interesting things that happened when you arrived. | When we arrived, we …<br>First of all … | |
| *Next events* | Tell the reader all the interesting things that followed – in the order they happened.<br><br>Start a new paragraph for each new event. | After that we …<br>Then we …<br>Next we …<br>Furthermore we …<br>In addition we … | |
| *Concluding paragraph* | Summarise – pick out the main points of the trip.<br><br>Evaluate – tell the reader what was most significant or interesting. | *Summary* – At/by the end of the trip we learned/felt/thought….<br>*Evaluation* – The most interesting thing was …<br>The part we liked best was … | |

# SUCCESS SHEET 2: RECOUNT WRITING (NON-FICTION: TRIPS AND VISITS) *How well have I done?*

| Features | Have I thought about? | YES/NO | Notes for redrafting |
|---|---|---|---|
| *Title* | Does my title tell the reader what the recount is about in no more than eight words? | | |
| *Overview paragraph* | Have I written my overview paragraph in the past tense?<br><br>Does it tell the reader<br>• When the trip happened?<br>• Who was involved?<br>• Where it happened?<br>• Why it happened?<br>• What you did?<br><br>Have I covered two or more of the above points in one sentence? | | |
| *Event 1* | Have I told the reader about my planning and preparation. e.g. reading books, searching the internet? Is what I have written relevant and interesting for the reader? | | |
| *Event 2* | Have I told the reader the first interesting things that happened when we arrived? | | |
| *Next events* | Have I told the reader all the interesting things that followed – in the order they happened?<br><br>Have I started a new paragraph for each new event? | | |
| *Concluding paragraph* | Which ending have I chosen?<br>– *summary* (picking out the main points of the trip)<br>OR *evaluation* (telling the reader what was most significant or interesting)? | | |

# SUCCESS SHEET 1: RECOUNT WRITING (BIOGRAPHY): *Ideas draft*

| Features | Think about! | Example | My own examples |
|---|---|---|---|
| *Title* | Your title should tell the reader who the biography is about in no more than eight words. | The Life of Gandhi | |
| *Overview paragraph* | Your overview paragraph should follow this order:<br>1 Who is it about and what are they best known for?<br>2 When did they live?<br>3 Where did they live?<br>4 Why are they important?<br><br>Answer two or more of the questions in one sentence. | Gandhi (*who*) was a great Indian leader (*main achievement*). He was born in 1869 and died in 1948 (*when*). As a child he lived in West India, then studied in London, and worked in South Africa (*where*), before returning to India at the age of 45 (*when*). He is famous for his peaceful, non violent approach to politics (*why he is important*). | |
| *Childhood events* | Include any childhood events you think are important. | When he was a child Gandhi saw …<br>As a child he … | |
| *Early life, events and achievements* | Tell the reader the important things which happened in the person's early life and perhaps how these influenced his/her later work. | In his early life Gandhi worked as / studied / visited / saw / experienced / thought … | |
| *Later life, events and achievements* | Tell the reader the important things which happened in the person's later life. Tell the events in the order in which they happened. Indicate whether their later life achievements are more or less important than the earlier ones. | As Gandhi grew older, he …<br>In later life he … | |
| *Concluding paragraph* | Tell the reader the importance or impact of what the person did during his/her life; what we can learn from him/her; how s/he affected others. | Today Gandhi is remembered for …<br>The lesson we can learn ….<br>His life is interesting/important because … | |

43

# SUCCESS SHEET 2: RECOUNT WRITING (BIOGRAPHY): *How well have I done?*

| Features | Have I thought about? | Yes/No | Notes for redrafting |
|---|---|---|---|
| Title | Does my title tell the reader who my biography is about, in no more than eight words? | | |
| Overview paragraph | Does my paragraph follow this order:<br>• Who is it about and what is s/he best known for?<br>• When did s/he live?<br>• Where did s/he live?<br>• Why is s/he important?<br>Have I answered two or more of the above in one sentence? | | |
| Childhood events | Have I included the important events from his/her childhood? | | |
| Early life, events and achievements | Have I told the reader the important things which happened in their early life and how these influenced their later life? | | |
| Later life, events and achievements | Have I told the events in the order in which they happened?<br>Have I said which achievements were the most important? | | |
| Concluding paragraph | Have I told the reader the importance of what 'X' did during his/her life?<br>Have I told the reader what we can learn from him/her?<br>Or how s/he affected others? | | |

# SUCCESS SHEET 1: RECOUNT WRITING (HISTORICAL): *Ideas draft*

| Features | Think about! | Example | My own examples |
|---|---|---|---|
| *Title* | Your title should tell the reader what the historical recount is about in no more than eight words. | The Fire of London | |
| *Overview paragraph* | Write your overview paragraph in the past tense.<br><br>It should tell the reader<br>• When the events happened.<br>• Who was involved.<br>• Where it happened.<br>• Why it happened.<br>• What the consequences of the events were.<br>Answer two or more of the questions in one sentence. | The Fire of London began in Pudding Lane (*where*) on 1 September 1666 (*when*) and spread through the city for five days. The wooden buildings burned easily (*why*) causing a great deal of damage so that much of the city had to be rebuilt (*consequence*). | |
| *Events and their consequences in the order in which they happened* | Tell the reader the first interesting/exciting thing that happened.<br><br>Tell the reader the next things that happened, in the order in which they occurred.<br><br>Tell the reader what happened as a consequence of these events.<br><br>Start a new paragraph for each new event. | It all began on Saturday …<br>At first people were not too concerned …<br>Many left their homes …<br>The next day an easterly wind …<br>On Monday the king rode …<br>On Tuesday the fire reached St Paul's …<br>Fortunately on Wednesday the wind dropped and … | |
| *Concluding paragraph* | Tell the reader the end result of all that happened.<br><br>Indicate whether the end result was positive or negative.<br><br>*Evaluate* – tell the reader what was most significant or interesting in the events which happened. | *Result* – Much of the city was ruined by the fire but the rebuilt city was much better than the one it replaced. (positive)<br><br>*Evaluation* – The best result, however, was the fact that the fire destroyed any remaining traces of the plague, which had killed so many the previous year. | |

45

# SUCCESS SHEET 2: RECOUNT WRITING (HISTORICAL): *How well have I done?*

| Features | Have I thought about? | YES/NO | Notes for redrafting |
|---|---|---|---|
| *Title* | Does my title tell the reader what the historical recount is about in no more than eight words? | | |
| *Overview paragraph* | Have I written my overview paragraph in the past tense?<br><br>Does it tell the reader<br>• When the events happened?<br>• Who was involved?<br>• Where it happened?<br>• Why it happened?<br>• What the consequences of the events were?<br><br>Have I answered two or more of the questions in one sentence? | | |
| *Events and their consequences in the order in which they happened* | Have I told the reader the first interesting/exciting thing that happened?<br><br>Then the next things that happened, in the order in which they occurred?<br><br>Have I told the reader what happened as a consequence of these events?<br><br>Have I started a new paragraph for each new event? | | |
| *Concluding paragraph* | Have I told the reader the end result of all that happened?<br><br>Have I indicated whether the end result was positive or negative?<br><br>*Evaluate* – Have I told the reader what was most significant or interesting in the events which happened? | | |

# 3 Writing explanations

## 1 Definition

The purpose of an explanation is to say how something works, what causes something to happen, or when or where something takes place. Explanations are not simply descriptions since they provide reasons and analysis, and some link cause and effect. Explanations are extended pieces of writing which provide answers to questions such as how, why, when or where.

## 2 NLS Framework links

### Year 2 Term 2

- **T21** ' produce simple flow charts or diagrams that explain a process'

### Year 4 Term 2

- **T20** 'improve the cohesion of written explanations through paragraphing and the use of link phrases and organisational devices such as sub-headings and numbering'
- **T25** 'write explanations of a process, using conventions identified through reading'

### Year 5 Term 2

- **T22** 'plan, compose, edit and refine short explanatory texts, using reading as a source, focusing on clarity, conciseness and impersonal style'

## 3 Text level features (purpose and organisation)

*Organisation*

We suggest the following organisation is used when introducing pupils to writing explanations:
- Title (Usually beginning with *how* or *why*)
- General statement of the subject of the explanation
- Key points paragraphs – these paragraphs contain the key points of the explanation presented in logical sequence to explain how or why something works or happens.
- Summary paragraph

## 4 Sentence level features (style, punctuation and grammar)

*Style*
- use of appropriate language to link paragraphs sequentially, e.g. *firstly, secondly, furthermore, in addition*
- use of organisational devices such as sub-headings and numbering

*Punctuation*
- use of paragraphing to separate key points
- use of the colon prior to listing, e.g. 'There were three reasons why the Titanic sank: human error, striking an iceberg, and the tearing of a gash which affected all compartments.'
- use of commas to separate items in a list

*Grammar*
- consistent tense use – simple present tense in explanations of e.g. how things work, or the past tense in e.g. explanations of why things happened

## 5 Word level features (vocabulary, spelling)

*Vocabulary*
- use of causal connectives – e.g. *therefore, because, as a result of, consequently* etc.
- subject-specific words

*Spelling*
- *Firstly, secondly* etc.
- *Consequently, therefore, because* etc.
- Subject-specific words

## 6 Note-making and writing explanations

Explanations, more than other text forms, can be made more effective by the inclusion of plans, maps, charts or annotated diagrams, and pupils should be encouraged to use these where they will clarify or enhance the explanation. Simple explanations can be expressed in the form of a flow chart (see suggested Activity 2: Making a Flow Chart), but it becomes more difficult with more complex explanations, when, for example, a flow chart has to show how a number of things cause something to happen, or when it has to describe a process which is reversible, e.g. in science when heat is applied to a solid, changing it first to a liquid then a gas, then reverses the process by cooling.

It is appropriate when considering explanations of a process to teach (or remind pupils of) how to use headings and subheadings (see Success Sheet 1 of a process based on 'How a frog develops'). Similarly when considering explanations of how things work, the use of numbering is helpful (see 'Success Sheet 1: How Things Work' based on the eye).

To sum up: the following note-making techniques should be taught alongside explanation writing:
- flow charts
- headings and subheadings
- numbering points.

48

And a reminder of the suggestion that pupils gather information for their flow chart on separate cards so that they can arrange (and re-arrange if necessary) their notes effectively.

## 7 Teachers' notes

There are many opportunities for examining and writing explanations across the curriculum, e.g.:

- in science – how an electric circuit works, what happens when materials are mixed, why plants grow
- in history – how their local area has changed over time, what caused a war, why Henry VIII had six wives
- in geography – why a town developed, how two areas differ, the effects of erosion on our coastline
- in music – why a particular instrument produces a sound, how to play a musical instrument

*Recommended sequence of lessons*

1. Deconstruction of an existing explanation to match the writing objectives for the year group (Activity 1).
2. Years 2 and 3 – teacher models how to make a flow chart (see Activity 2).
3. However, if flow charts have not been covered in Years 2 and 3, or pupils require reinforcement of their understanding of the form, then this may also be an appropriate part of the lesson sequence for pupils in Years 4 and 5.
4. Next pupils make their own flow chart, either individually or in pairs or small groups. Depending on the nature and form of the explanation to be produced, this may or may not be appropriate for Years 4 and 5. This may be as far as the teacher takes the writing of an explanation with pupils in Years 2 and 3.
5. Teacher models how to organise the flow chart notes into an explanation (following the model outlined in Success Sheet 1) focusing on the key points highlighted during the deconstruction activity.
6. Following the model demonstrated by the teacher, pupils plan their own explanation using Success Sheet 1 and write their first draft.
7. Pupils evaluate their explanation using Success Sheet 2.
8. Teacher provides feedback to pupils on their explanations and evaluations – this can be done orally or in writing, as appropriate to the age/stage of development of their pupils.
9. Teacher summarises what has been learned about this text form with class.

Activities 3, 4 and 5 are additional activities which could be undertaken with pupils in Years 4, 5 or 6. The activities provide opportunities to improve the cohesion of texts by the use of link phrases (Activity 3), paragraphing (Activity 4) and organisational devices.

*Using the Success Sheets*

Teachers should note that the third item listed in the Features column on the Success Sheets is optional. It is not always appropriate in an explanation to classify or define the parts. When writing how a machine or a part of the human body works it is possible to isolate component parts, but this is not the case when explaining how or why something happens or happened.

Three versions of the Success Sheets have been provided at the end of the chapter:
1  explanations of a process
2  how things work
3  why something happened.

The three versions are similar and teachers should select the one which best suits the writing task they have selected for the class.

When pupils have created a flow chart as a preliminary to writing their explanation, teachers may wish to produce an enlarged version of Success Sheet 1: Ideas Draft so that pupils can use the flow chart notes to write their first draft directly.

When the pupils are writing the Key Points section of their explanation, the teacher may wish to cross-reference to page 23 in the chapter on Writing Instructions, as the language sequence model identified there is also appropriate for explanations.

## 8  Activity suggestions

*Activity 1: Deconstructing an explanation*

Teachers can use the example given, page 54) as a vehicle for identifying the key features of writing an explanation (at text, sentence and word level) with their class or group.

*Activity 2: Making a flow chart*

The text used for Activity 1 could be used to demonstrate a simple flowchart:

Teachers may then wish to demonstrate the creation of a more complex flow chart to explain what happens to an egg from being laid to being used in cooking, e.g.

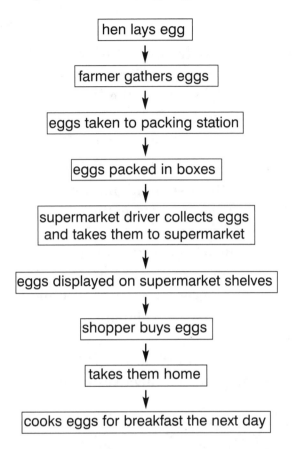

hen lays egg
↓
farmer gathers eggs
↓
eggs taken to packing station
↓
eggs packed in boxes
↓
supermarket driver collects eggs and takes them to supermarket
↓
eggs displayed on supermarket shelves
↓
shopper buys eggs
↓
takes them home
↓
cooks eggs for breakfast the next day

Alternative layouts for the flow chart, and when they might be appropriate, could be discussed, e.g.

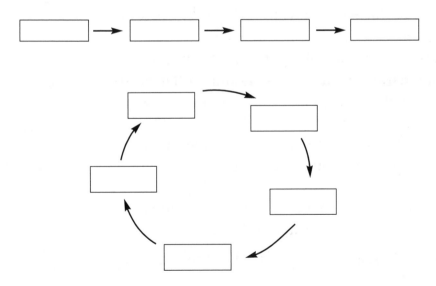

Pupils in Years 2 and 3 would now complete their own flow chart. This could follow the example of the egg (e.g. picking, canning, cooking tomatoes) or the flow chart could relate something the pupils are doing in another curricular area, such as what happens to a seed from planting to flowering. Pupils in Years 4 and 5 would be asked to complete a flow chart relating to the explanation they are going to write.

*Activity 3: Linking words and phrases*

On page 56 is a piece of writing entitled 'Why animals in the wild are in danger', but it lacks the linking words and phrases that would make the explanation clear, by showing the connections between the ideas. The suggested organisation for this lesson is as follows:

1. Pupils are issued with copies of the text and asked to add in linking words or phrases to improve this explanation. The teacher should tell the class that they can rearrange the text if they feel it helps to improve the explanation.
2. Teacher leads discussion of the merits of different choices of linking words/phrases, focusing attention on the use of temporal and causal connectives. The class (or group) working with the teacher produce a well-linked clear explanation of why the animals are in danger.
3. This could be displayed as a 'Before and After' poster, with annotation of the changes highlighting the connectives used.

*Activity 4: Paragraphing an explanation text*

The text used for this activity (page 57) is an explanation of the process of growing tea for export. The suggested organisation for a lesson on paragraphing a text is as follows:

1. The teacher uses an information text to remind the class of the purpose of paragraphs.
2. Pairs of pupils are given a copy of this text and asked to indicate where the paragraph divisions should be. There are six or seven paragraphs in the text, broadly indicating the different stages in the process.
3. When this is completed, two pairs link up, compare their choice of divisions and reach agreement on the paragraphing of the text.
4. The teacher leads a class review of the correct divisions, emphasising the purpose of paragraph divisions.

The NLS Framework 'Glossary of Terms used in the Framework', states (page 84):

*Paragraph*

*A section or piece of writing. A new paragraph marks a change of focus, a change of time, a change of place or a change of speaker in a passage of dialogue.*

*A new paragraph begins on a new line usually with a one line gap separating it from the previous paragraph.*

*Paragraphing helps writers to organise their thoughts and helps readers to follow the story line, argument or dialogue.*

We think that paragraphing also helps the reader to follow the line of thought or the sequential development of an argument in non-fiction writing.

The passage should be divided into paragraphs at the following points (please note that it would also be acceptable to divide the final paragraph and begin a new paragraph at 'The tea is then packed', making seven paragraphs in total):

*Since tea is damaged by frost, it is usually grown in countries with a warm climate ...*

*The young tea plants are grown in nurseries, protected from the sun by bamboo frames ...*

*Many insect pests attack the tea bushes ...*

*When the tea plant is sufficiently grown, it is transplanted from the nurseries into the main fields ...*

*Full baskets of leaves are taken to a nearby factory where the tender leaves are spread on racks to dry or wither ...*

*The leaves are then fermented in a special cool damp room ...*

*Activity 5: Sequencing an explanation text*

The next text example (pages 58 and 59) explains what happened to the *Hindenburg* (with an alternative text on evacuation in the Second World War). This is used for a lesson in sequencing the paragraphs in a text. The suggested organisation for this lesson is as follows:

1. The paragraphs of this text are separated onto cards (one card for each paragraph).
2. Pupils work in pairs to place the paragraphs in the correct order.
3. Pairs can be linked up to compare their selection and reach agreement, prior to the teacher conducting a review of the correct sequence.
4. The teacher-led review considers the structure of this explanation text and relates this to the structural model we have proposed in the Success Sheets.
5. An extension (or alternative) activity would be to ask pupils to provide sub-headings for the text to show how they can help to make an explanation even clearer.

# Butterfly Eggs → Caterpillars → Butterfly

## Butterfly Eggs

- A Butterfly egg is a soft white blob which lies down on a leaf
- It lies on a leaf until it's time to hatch. It looks a bit like a jellybean.
- Every butterfly starts his or hers life as a small, warm, white eggs

## Caterpillars lose their →

- caterpillars lose their first skin and they grow another four times.
- They crack a hole in the shell of the egg. when it's hatched
- It then scuttles it's way up a tree and eats a small hole in the leaf
- The caterpillar crawls around looking for food and get bigger and fatter.
- It then spins a pupa around itself.

## Butterfly

- The Butterfly come out of the pupa until its wings and waits are dry.
- A butterfly is an insect and it flys about until it finds a flower to land on.
- They love fluttering around playing with there brothers and sisters.
- They are all beautiful colours or maybe multicoloured.
- Butterflies fly from flower to flower collecting nector.
- When the butterflies hatch more butterflies arrive in our world.

*Example of a Year 2 pupil's explanation text, 'How a butterfly develops'.*

| | Title | # How a frog develops | |
|---|---|---|---|
| **General statement** | | A frog is an amphibian with webbed feet and no tail. There are 2,770 known species of frog found throughout the world. The cycle that takes them from the egg to adulthood can take from 2 months to 2 years, depending on the species and its habitat. | *This paragraph explains what the frog is and the fact that there are a large number of species.* |
| **Parts** | | The life cycle of the frog consists of three main stages: the egg, the tadpole and the adult frog. | *This paragraph indicates the 3 stages in the life cycle.* |
| **Key point paragraphs** | | **Stage 1: The Egg**<br>Female frogs lay anything from 19 to 30,000 eggs. Because frogs' eggs are a favourite of many predators, laying eggs in large numbers ensures that at least some hatch out. Eggs are laid in water and they are covered in an envelope of jelly-like substance. This is called frog spawn.<br><br>**Stage 2: The Tadpole**<br>When the tadpole has had enough time to develop in the egg, the egg begins to break up, allowing the tadpole to emerge. The tadpole quickly develops a long tail which helps it to move about in the water.<br><br>**Stage 3: The Adult Frog**<br>The tadpole gradually changes. Hind legs begin to appear, then forelegs. The process of change can take from 12 days to 3 years depending on the species. Finally the frog is fully developed. The tail has disappeared and the frog is ready to live on the surface. | *Note how numbering and subheadings have been used to clarify the three stages of the life cycle.* |
| **Summary paragraph** | | After some time the new frog will be old enough to start breeding and the cycle begins again. | *The important point being made is the fact that the cycle continues with each new frog.* |

# Why animals in the wild are in danger
## Animals losing their homes

Rainforests grow in warm, wet countries. Lots of animals live in them. There are chimpanzees and sun birds in African rainforests. There are tigers and peacocks in the Indian rainforest. In all of them there are many varieties of snakes, frogs and insects. Forests are being cut down all over the world and many of them are rain forests.

Half the rainforests in the world have gone. There are fewer than 4,000 orang-utans left in the world. Their homes in the rainforest have been cut down.

The roots of trees hold soil in place. Trees are cut down. Rain washes soil away. This is called erosion. Rainwater carries the soil down rivers to the sea. The soil settles at the mouth of the river and blocks it. Sometimes there is flooding.

People need land to grow food. They cut down the trees. They spray the land with weedkiller. The weeds die. Insects, and the birds which eat them, have nowhere to live. They put up fences and wild animals like deer and buffalo can no longer search for food. There were millions of bison. Only a few are left.

# How tea is produced

Since tea is damaged by frost, it is usually grown in countries with a warm climate. Tea plants also need plenty of rain and well-drained soil. This is why the best tea is grown on high land in the tropics where the air is cooler. The three countries which are the largest producers of tea are India, Sri Lanka and China. The young tea plants are grown in nurseries, protected from the sun by bamboo frames. In China and Japan tea is grown in small patches on steep hillsides which are unsuitable for other crops. In other countries it is grown on plantations. Many insect pests attack the tea bushes. The worst disease of tea is called blister blight. This is caused by a fungus which can be controlled by special sprays. When the tea plant is sufficiently grown, it is transplanted from the nurseries into the main fields. It is pruned and trained to grow into a small bush. Without pruning it would grow into a tree about 15 metres high. Tea plants must grow for five years before the leaves are ready for plucking. When the plants are ready the top two leaves and a bud from each stalk are plucked. Full baskets of leaves are taken to a nearby factory where the tender leaves are spread on racks to dry or wither. Hot air is blown under and up through the tea leaves. A rolling machine squeezes out any juices left by crushing the leaves. The leaves are then fermented in a special cool damp room. They take in oxygen from the air and turn a brown rusty colour. Fermentation is stopped after two to four hours by passing the tea through the hot air of a firing machine. Now the tea has become the black dry leaf that we know. The tea is then packed in special tea chests and taken by cart, lorry, train or boat to the nearest seaport, from where they are exported.

# What happened to the Hindenberg?

The Hindenburg was a huge German airship built in 1936 by the Zeppelin company. It was 50 metres high and 250 metres long. The framework was made of a light alloy of aluminium and copper and the outside was covered with cotton fabric and then coated with silver paint to protect it from the sun and rain. The ship was hollow inside. The hydrogen used to make it float was contained in 16 gas bags. These were made of specially treated cotton fabric.

Passengers on the Hindenburg spent their journey in hotel-style luxury. The airship was a very safe way to travel, except for the fact that it contained hydrogen. Hydrogen, when mixed with air and ignited, explodes violently. Rigorous safety precautions were taken on board the Hindenburg to prevent the hydrogen being set on fire.

On 3 May 1937 the Hindenburg left Frankfurt for Lakehurst, Chicago. On board were thirty six passengers and sixty one crew members. They were delayed by head winds and did not reach Lakehurst till late afternoon. As the airship prepared to land, hundreds of onlookers gathered to watch. At 19.21 they began landing procedures.

Suddenly the airship burst into flame at an altitude of about 200 feet and in a matter of seconds it came down in a fiery blaze. Passengers and crewmen made desperate efforts to escape from the burning airship. Some jumped while they were still 30 metres above the ground. Some waited till the framework had fallen and tried to fight their way out through the white-hot metal. Many were trapped and burned before they could get away from the ship.

Out of the ninety-seven people on board, thirty five lost their lives, thirteen passengers and twenty-two crewmen. Germany's record for airship safety was shattered and, because of this terrible disaster, people lost their faith in airships as a means of transporting passengers.

What caused the disaster? Sabotage? A bolt of lightning? Nobody really knew until recently. A NASA scientist has found proof that the fabric used for the outer skin was to blame. A single spark of static electricity was enough to make it burn like dry leaves. German engineers had designed a flying bomb just waiting to explode.

# What happened to children who were evacuated?

A few days before the Second World War broke out, thousands of schoolchildren were moved from their homes in towns and cities into the country, Parents knew the cities were far more likely to be bombed than the countryside, and they wanted their children to be as safe as possible. The children went to stay with foster parents. People called billeting officers had the job of seeing that all the children had somewhere to stay.

All the children in a school were evacuated together, with their teachers, so that the school could be set up in the country.

Evacuees travelled by bus or train and were usually taken to a local hall and the foster parents arrived to collect them. They looked at the children and picked out the ones they liked. Big boys were often chosen by farmers because they would be able to help on the farm. If the evacuees were girls, the older ones were usually picked first because they could help with the housework. Many people would only take one evacuee, but the billeting officer sometimes persuaded them to take two. Some took an extra child because their chosen evacuee had a brother or sister and refused to leave them. Foster parents were given a small sum of money each week in return for looking after an evacuee.

City children found life in the country strange. Many children wet their beds because they were frightened at being in a strange place, and got into trouble with their foster parents. Many evacuees were homesick and missed their parents and family. When it became clear that they were not going to settle down, many parents, unable to bear seeing their children so miserable, decided to bring them home. During the 'Phoney War' period about three quarters of all evacuees returned to their homes.

*from Daily Life in a Wartime House by Laura Wilson*

# SUCCESS SHEET 1: WRITING EXPLANATIONS (OF A PROCESS): *Ideas draft*

| Features | Think about! | Example | My own examples |
|---|---|---|---|
| *Title* | Tell the reader what the explanation is about. | How a frog develops | |
| *General statement (what the explanation is about)* | Introduce the reader to the subject of the explanation. (Perhaps by saying what it is a part of or what it belongs to) | How a frog develops from an egg in frogspawn into an adult frog. | |
| *Parts (OPTIONAL) (This may be linked to the general statement)* | Tell the reader the different parts that make up the subject. (NB This paragraph is optional – you don't have to include it if it doesn't work easily with your subject) | There are three main stages in the development of a frog: the egg, the tadpole and the adult frog. | |
| *Key Points paragraphs* | Tell the reader how it works or what happens. Select the important points. You may wish to use sub-headings or numbering to organise your key points. | First Stage: The Egg<br>First of all …<br>Female frogs lay …<br>The reason they lay so many …<br><br>Stage 2: The Tadpole<br>The next thing that happens is …<br>When the egg has fully developed …<br>Then …<br>• long tail for moving in water<br>• begins to develop legs<br><br>Stage 3: The Adult Frog<br>Finally the frog is fully developed …<br>• tail disappears<br>• front and back legs<br>• can live on land | |
| *Summary paragraph* | Tell the reader something special or important about the subject | After some time this new frog will be old enough to start breeding and the cycle can continue. | |

60

# SUCCESS Sheet 2: EXPLANATIONS (OF A PROCESS): *How well have I done?*

| Features | Have I thought about? | YES/NO | Notes for redrafting |
|---|---|---|---|
| Title | Have I told the reader what the explanation is about? | | |
| General statement (what the explanation is about) | Have I introduced the reader to the subject of the explanation? | | |
| Parts (OPTIONAL) (This may be linked to the general statement) | Have I told the reader the different parts that make up the subject? | | |
| Key Points paragraphs | Have I told the reader how it works or what happens? Have I covered all the important points? Have I used sub-headings or numbering to organise my key points? | | |
| Summary paragraph | Have I told the reader something special or important about the subject? | | |

# SUCCESS SHEET 1: WRITING EXPLANATIONS (HOW THINGS WORK): *Ideas draft*

| Features | Think about! | Example | My own examples |
|---|---|---|---|
| *Title* | Tell the reader what the explanation is about. | How the human eye works | |
| *General statement (what the explanation is about)* | Introduce the reader to the subject of the explanation. (Perhaps by saying what it is a part of or what it belongs to) | • most important part of the human body because it enables humans to see | |
| *Parts (OPTIONAL) (This may be linked to the general statement)* | Tell the reader the different parts that make up the subject. (NB This paragraph is optional – you don't have to include it if it doesn't work easily with your subject) Would a diagram help? | • very complex<br>• contains the cornea, pupil, iris, lens etc<br>Include annotated diagram of the eye to show how it works | |
| *Key Points paragraphs* | Tell the reader how it works. Select the important points. You may wish to use sub-headings or numbering to organise your key points. Use sequencing words such as *firstly, next* etc. | It works in the following way:<br>First of all …<br>Next/secondly …<br>After that/thirdly …<br>And as a result …<br><br>The way each part works is as follows:<br>1 The cornea …<br>2 The pupil …<br>3 The iris … etc. | |
| *Summary paragraph* | Tell the reader something special or important about the subject | Without sight humans would have one sense less to rely upon. Our eyes are therefore very special and should be taken care of. | |

# SUCCESS SHEET 2: EXPLANATIONS (HOW THINGS WORK): *How well have I done?*

| Features | Have I thought about? | YES/NO | Notes for redrafting |
|---|---|---|---|
| Title | Have I told the reader what the explanation is about? | | |
| General statement (what the explanation is about) | Have I introduced the reader to the subject of the explanation? (Perhaps by saying what it is a part of or what it belongs to) | | |
| Parts (OPTIONAL) (This may be linked to the general statement) | Have I told the reader the different parts that make up the subject? Have I used a diagram? | | |
| Key Points paragraphs | Have I told the reader how it works? Have I selected the important points? Have I used sub-headings or numbering to organise my key points? If not, would they make my explanation clearer? Have I used sequencing words such as firstly, next etc? | | |
| Summary paragraph | Have I told the reader something special or important about the subject? | | |

# SUCCESS SHEET 1: WRITING EXPLANATIONS (WHY SOMETHING HAPPENED): *Ideas draft*

| Features | Think about! | Example | My own examples |
|---|---|---|---|
| *Title* | Tell the reader what the explanation is about. | Why the *Titanic* sank | |
| *General statement (what the explanation is about)* | Introduce the reader to the subject of the explanation. (Perhaps by saying what it is a part of or what it belongs to.) | I want to explain why the Titanic, which was supposed to be unsinkable, sank in the North Atlantic with the loss of so many lives. | |
| *Introductory paragraph* | Set the scene for the reader. Select the important points. | The ship set sail to cross the Atlantic on …<br>• maiden voyage<br>• beginning all went well<br>• then ship struck iceberg | |
| *Key Points paragraphs* | You may wish to use sub-headings or numbering to organise your key points.<br><br>Use linking phrases such as 'the main reason is …', 'a further reason is …', etc. | The main reason is …<br>Another reason is …<br>It sank very quickly – reasons:<br>• moving quickly<br>• couldn't manoeuvre quickly<br>• iceberg did a lot of damage<br>• bulkheads filled with water quickly<br>• unbalanced, ship began to tip<br>• inferior construction – not built to stand up to low temperatures<br>• …<br>In addition, the reasons so many lives were lost are …<br>• not enough lifeboats<br>• people panicked<br>• … | |
| *Summary paragraph* | Sum up for the reader why this happened. | So you can see why … | |

# SUCCESS SHEET 2: EXPLANATIONS (WHY SOMETHING HAPPENED) *How well have I done?*

| Features | Have I thought about? | YES/NO | Notes for redrafting |
|---|---|---|---|
| *Title* | Have I told the reader what the explanation is about? | | |
| *General statement (what the explanation is about)* | Have I introduced the reader to the subject of the explanation? (Perhaps by saying what it is a part of or what it belongs to) | | |
| *Introductory paragraph* | Have I set the scene with the reader? | | |
| *Key Points paragraphs* | Have I selected the important points? Have I used sub-headings or numbering to organise my key points? Have I used linking phrases such as 'the main reason is …', 'a further reason is …' etc? | | |
| *Summary paragraph* | Have I summed up for the reader why this has happened? Or provided a neat conclusion? | | |

# 4 Writing reports

## 1 Definition

A report is an account of a wide range of natural, cultural or social phenomena, often made as a result of an investigation which has been carried out. At its most basic, a report consists of the systematic organisation of factual information which has been gathered. Report writing is probably the most common cross-curricular form of non-fiction writing which pupils are asked to produce, and subjects such as science, design technology, history, geography, art and music provide real contexts for this form of writing.

## 2 NLS Framework links

### Year 2 Term 3

- **T21** 'to write non-chronological reports based on structure of known texts, e.g. *There are two sorts of x …; They live in x …; the A's have x … but the B's etc*, using appropriate language to present, sequence and categorise ideas'

### Year 3 Term 1

- **T21** 'to make a simple record of information from texts read, e.g. by completing a chart of information discovered, by listing keywords, drawing together notes from more than one source'
- **T22** 'to write simple non-chronological reports from known information e.g. from own experience or from texts read, using notes made to organise and present ideas. Write for a known audience, e.g. other pupils in class, teacher, parent'

### Year 4 Term 1

- **T27** 'to write a non-chronological report, including the use of organisational devices, e.g. numbered lists, headings for conciseness by: generalising some of the details; deleting the least important details'

### Year 5 Term 1

- **T22** 'to plan, compose, edit and refine short non-chronological reports and explanatory texts, using reading as a source, focusing on clarity, conciseness and impersonal style'
- **T23** 'to record and acknowledge sources in their own writing'

### Year 6 Term 1

- **T22** 'to write non-chronological reports linked to other subjects'

## 3 Text level features (purpose and organisation)

The main purpose of report writing is to produce a systematic organisation of factual information, which has often been gathered as a result of an investigation in order to inform the reader.

In this chapter we group reports under the following headings:
- factual reports
- reports based on comparing and contrasting different phenomena.

We have divided this chapter into two sections, A and B. Section A deals with factual reports and Section B deals with reports involving comparison.

## 4 Sentence level features (style, punctuation and grammar)

*Style*
- based on facts
- omission of opinions
- formal and objective
- non-chronological

*Punctuation*
- use of paragraphs to separate key points
- use of colon for listing e.g. *There are many different kinds of spider: tarantula, black widow, bird-eating*
- use of commas to separate items on a list

*Grammar* (when developing impersonal style in Years 5 and 6)
- use of the continuous present tense e.g. *The structure of spiders' webs is being used to help with building design.*
- no use of I/we

## 5 Word level features (vocabulary, spelling)

*Vocabulary*
- use of subject-specific words, including scientific vocabulary
- language of classification e.g. *belongs to, is part of*
- language of comparison and contrast e.g. *resembles, similar, different, like*
- factual rather than imaginative language

*Spelling*
- *furthermore, in addition, moreover* etc.
- *comparable, resembles, alike, contrasting, dissimilar, different* etc.
- subject specific words (see Activities 1 and 2 in Chapter 3)

# 6 Note-making and writing reports

The production of a successful report depends upon research and the ability to handle information effectively. In terms of writing reports this means pupils need to be able to:

- locate the information required to write their report
- evaluate the accuracy and relevance of information they find
- select what they need for their report and make notes
- organise their notes and plan the report
- write the report

(See Appendix 1 on research and note-making skills for further information)

NLF Reading and Writing objectives for Years 2 and 3 indicate that many of the necessary research and note-making skills should be taught with these year groups. (See Appendix 2, progression chart, page 172)

The organisation of information before the production of a final report is vital. For this reason we recommend that teachers encourage their pupils to :

1 create spider diagrams to frame their research

2 complete an information recording grid to organise their information under different  headings.

# 7 Teachers' notes

There are many opportunities for writing reports across the curriculum:

- reporting historical events, comparing and contrasting aspects of life in different periods in history
- describing geographical features, comparing different areas in geography
- describing what happens during an investigation, how different plants and animals respond to their different environments, comparing and contrasting the effects of light on different surfaces in science
- comparing and contrasting the work of different artists or musicians

## Section A: Factual reports

As with all forms of writing, the most important thing is that pupils have a clear idea of purpose and audience for any reports they are writing: this is crucial. If pupils have a clear understanding of the purpose of the report they are more likely to adopt an appropriate tone in conveying the information to the reader (See Activity 4).

The bulk of any report is made up of the key features relating to the subject of the report. We recommend that, before using the Information Recording Grids and Success Sheets, teachers consider which key features are relevant to the subject of the report to be written by their pupils (as pertinent features will vary from subject to subject) and discuss these with their pupils. Alternatively the key features could be the subject of a brainstorming session (See Activity 1).

A particular teaching point to emphasise is the need to explain clearly how to use Information Recording Grids (page 77) before using Success Sheet 1: Ideas Draft (page 92). Blank spaces have been included in the features box in the Factual Report Information Recording Grid so that pupils can add any features relevant to their subject, not previously included on the grid. In many cases the use of an information recording grid may make the use of Success Sheet 1: Ideas Draft unnecessary (see Activity 2).

Teachers should also draw attention to 'Significance' in the Key Features column, as this encourages pupils to engage in the process of evaluating the relative importance of the information retrieved or gathered.

The planning stage is of vital importance to the process of writing effective reports as it gives pupils a visual grasp of the structure of the whole. As information retrieved is often drawn from a broad range of sources, this approach reduces the possibility of a disorganised, diffuse series of notes which are hard to structure further.

When transferring information from the Information Recording Grids to the first draft of a report, teachers may wish to discuss the possibility of re-ordering key features so that they appear in the first draft (or on Success Sheet 1) in a sequence which is different from that presented on the Information Recording Grid, e.g. one method of selection is to choose the feature for which there is most information and place this first in the draft in order to provide an in-depth opening to the report. Another method is to select the most significant key feature and then use this in the penultimate ('Significance') paragraph. The crucial teaching point is to make pupils aware that they have choices and that they should have sound reasons for the choices they make.

We suggest the following organisation for factual reports:
• Title
• Clarification/context statement paragraph

- Key features
- Significance
- Summary statement

*Recommended sequence of lessons*

1 Brainstorm the subject for the report and create a spider diagram (Activity 1).

2 Model how to complete an Information Grid for factual reports (Activity 2).

3 Deconstruction of an existing report (Activity 3).

4 Pupils complete an Information Recording Grid for their report.

5 Following the model demonstrated by the teacher, pupils plan their own report using Success Sheet 1 and write their first draft.

6 Pupils evaluate their report using Success Sheet 2.

7 Teacher provides feedback to pupils on their reports and evaluations – this can be done orally or in writing, as appropriate to the age/stage of development of their pupils.

8 Teacher leads an examination of an existing report written by a pupil, and discusses how the style is improved by choosing more formal and objective language (Activity 4).

9 Teacher completes an Information Recording Grid with the class or group, possibly related to a study taking place in another curricular area. The completed grid is given to the pupils to use as the starting point for writing their report (Activity 5).

10 Teacher summarises what has been learned about this text form with the class.

## 8 Factual Reports: Activity suggestions

*Activity 1: Creating a spider diagram*

The purpose of this activity is to brainstorm which aspects of the chosen topic might be researched in preparation for writing a report on that particular topic. The topic selected here is spiders but it can be any topic selected by the teacher, possibly one linked to current study in another curricular area. The teacher leads a brainstorming session and records the pupils' suggestions in the form of a spider diagram (see page 76).

*Activity 2: Using an Information Recording Grid*

The teacher should begin by discussing the blank proforma for an information grid, using an enlarged display version (see page 77). It is essential that pupils understand the various headings under the 'Key features' column and that they are clear how they can use the blank boxes on the grid.

The teacher then models for the class how the Information Recording Grid is completed (see page 78), highlighting the headings which have been added to match the information to be researched and the link with the spider diagram which was created from the initial brainstorm. (The completed version may have to be adjusted in the light of that brainstorming session.)

*Activity 3: Deconstructing a report*

Teachers can use the example given (see page 79) as a vehicle for discussion of the key features of this text form. As can be seen it relates directly to the subject of the brainstorm and the information completed on the information recording grid, used in Activities 1 and 2.

*Activity 4: Comparing two reports*

The teacher leads a discussion of two reports on spiders written by the same Year 5 pupil (one before using the SUCCESS Approach and one after), focusing on how the report has been improved and what effect more formal and objective language would have on the report (see pages 80 and 81).

*Activity 5: Using an Information Recording Grid (2)*

We would also recommend that on some occasions teachers work with their class or group to complete an Information Recording Grid. They then give the completed grid to the pupils who use it as the starting point for their report writing. Pupils could be asked to complete the first draft of their report on an enlarged version of Success Sheet 1.

Once pupils have completed their reports, the teacher leads a discussion during which the class or group look at a selection of different outcomes. Points for discussion could be:
• Which of the pupil outcomes has used the information provided best?
• Which report demonstrates the best organisation of the information?
• Which report has greatest impact? Why?

Such discussion will reinforce understanding of the text form and help to develop pupils' skills in looking critically at their own writing.

An example of an adapted Information Recording Grid for a factual report is included (see page 82). This demonstrates how the basic grid can be adapted for use in a specific context, in this case a report to be produced after growing a plant in class, as part of a science activity.

Two reports by Rebecca Jones, a Year 4 pupil, are shown here (pages 83–4). The first report was written before she tried the SUCCESS Approach, the second after, showing improved organisation and greater detail.

## Section B: Reports involving comparing/contrasting

*Organisation*

We suggest three different patterns of organisation for reports in which items are compared and/or contrasted which teachers may wish to use:

Type 1
- Title
- Context statement paragraph
- Similarity 1 paragraph
- Similarity 2 paragraph
- Further similarities paragraph(s)
- Difference 1 paragraph
- Difference 2 paragraph
- Further differences paragraph(s)
- Summary statement

Type 2
- Title
- Context statement paragraph
- Similarity 1 paragraph
- Difference 1 paragraph
- Similarity 2 paragraph
- Difference 2 paragraph
- Further similarities and differences paragraph(s)
- Summary statement

Type 3
- Title
- Context statement paragraph
- Similarity and differences for first aspect of the subjects
- Similarity and differences for second aspect of the subjects

- Similarity and differences for third aspect of the subjects
- Further similarities and differences paragraphs as required by the subject
- Summary statement

## 9 Teachers' notes: reports involving comparing and contrasting

The structure of a report depends on the purpose for which it is written. Comparison reports are often produced in order to provide a more rounded or contextualised understanding of the subject. For example, when comparing a past historical period with the present, the outcome is often a better understanding of the merits of both time frames. Likewise, a comparison of two disparate geographical areas can lead to greater understanding of both.

Teachers will note that we have chosen not to state an upper limit to the number of words in the title ( as we do for other forms), as the title length depends on the number of 'items' being compared e.g.
- A comparison of farming in East Anglia and the Lake District
- Comparing different aspects of life in Tudor times with life today.

Teachers may also wish to consider producing a Similarities Report for two (apparently) dissimilar things. The benefits of this relate to synectics; an aspect of synectics (connecting both hemispheres of the brain, thereby improving brain functioning) is the comparison of the dissimilar. The unusual nature of this activity can be a useful way of engaging more able pupils.

Pupils will have already been made aware of the importance of planning and making notes before writing a report. They should now be shown how the way in which an Information Recording Grid is completed can assist them in organising their report. It is, therefore, important that over time pupils are given opportunities to experience different types of organisation as they write different reports.

As you will have noted, we outlined three possible forms of text organisation for reports which compare and/or contrast. Types 1–3 are simply different ways in which reports involving comparing and contrasting items can be organised and pupils in the upper years should be introduced, over time, to all three forms of organisation, so that eventually they decide which is the most effective form of text organisation for the report they are writing. Check the exemplification of these different forms of text organisation in the relevant Success Sheets included at the end of this chapter:

- Type 1 organisation – grouping all the 'similarities' paragraphs which are then followed by all the 'differences' paragraphs.
- Type 2 organisation – alternating paragraphs for similarities and differences.
- Type 3 organisation – comparing and contrasting within the same paragraph.

*Recommended sequence of lessons*

This sequence of lessons assumes that pupils will have been involved in writing straightforward factual reports before they attempt to write reports in which items are compared and contrasted. Therefore some of the earlier sequence of lessons will already have been completed. This sequence may be repeated in full or in part to offer pupils experience of the three different types of text organisation. Teachers should feel free to provide their own examples which are more relevant to texts they are reading with the class or work being covered in other areas of the curriculum.

1 Teacher models how to complete an Information Recording Grid for compare & contrast reports using one of the exemplars, Type 1, 2 or 3.

2 Deconstruction of a 'compare & contrast' report, based on the exemplar chosen for lesson 1 in this sequence. Teachers should demonstrate the relationship between the way in which information has been recorded on an information grid and the final report produced.

3 Activity 6 offers an optional additional activity based on recording information on information grids.

4 The teacher introduces the subject pupils are to report on (perhaps linked to work currently taking place in another curricular area). Pupils carry out the necessary research and complete an information grid for their own report.

5 Following the model demonstrated by the teacher, pupils plan their own report, perhaps using Success Sheet 1, and write their first draft.

6 Pupils evaluate the first draft of their report using Success Sheet 2.

7 Teacher provides feedback to pupils on their reports and evaluations – this can be done orally or in writing, as appropriate to the age/stage of development of their pupils.

8 Teacher summarises what has been learned about this text form with class.

9 As stated earlier, parts of this sequence should be repeated on future occasions to ensure that pupils are introduced to the other types of text organisation. When all three have been covered, the next time pupils are required to write a report, the teacher should remind pupils of all three types of organisation and encourage them to choose the type of organisation they think best.

## 10 'Compare and contrast' reports: suggested activities

*Activity 6: Using an Information Recording Grid (3)*

The text extracts from 'When Hunger Calls' (page 85) provide an activity for taking notes using the Information Recording Grids provided (pages 86–7). As the original text consists of two separate paragraphs, pupils could be given the task of presenting their report using Type 3 organisation, i.e. comparing and contrasting different aspects within the same paragraph. The headings from the Information Recording Grid can provide the items to be covered in each paragraph, i.e. classification, location, hunting, prey etc.

Pages 88–91 show a Year 3 pupil's report writing – a report to children in the infant department (Year 2) to explain what it is like in the juniors.

# Factual report: Spider diagram

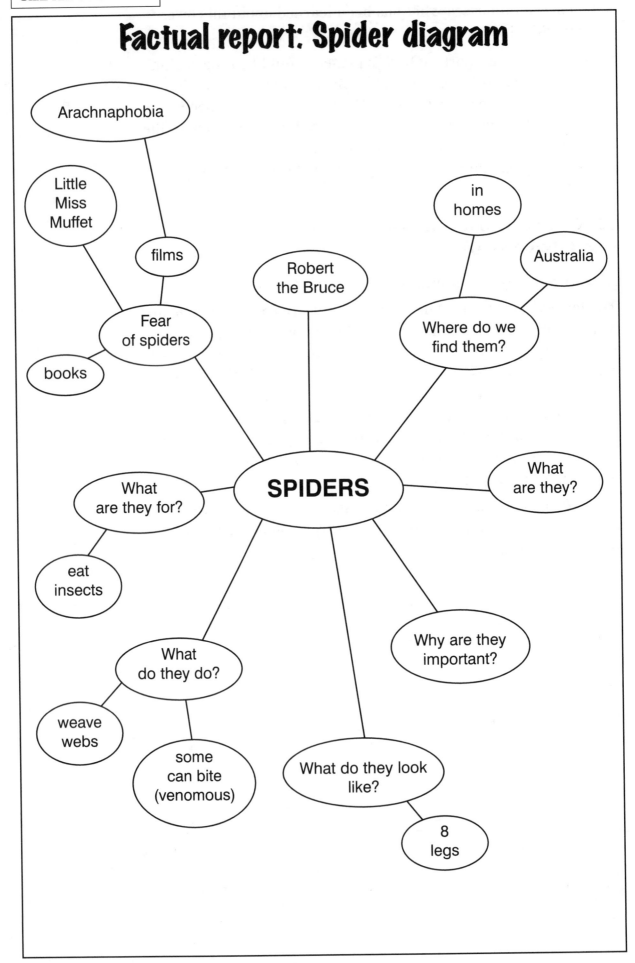

# Factual report: Information Recording Grid

**Title/subject of report:** _____

| KEY FEATURES | NOTES |
|---|---|
| CLASSIFICATION<br>What do they<br>belong to? | |
| APPEARANCE<br>What do they<br>look like? | |
| LOCATION<br>Where do you find<br>them? | |
| PURPOSE<br>What do they do?<br>What are they for? | |
| | |
| | |
| | |

# Factual report: Information Recording Grid

**Title/subject of report:** Spiders

| KEY FEATURES | NOTES |
|---|---|
| CLASSIFICATION (What do they belong to?) | • belong to arachnid family |
| APPEARANCE (What do they look like?) | • arthropods – hard external skeletons & jointed limbs<br>• narrow waist, 8 legs, can have 0, 2, 4, 6 etc. – 12 eyes<br>• have spinnerets in middle of abdomen |
| LOCATION (Where do you find them?) | • different species found in all countries around the world<br>• among earliest animals to live on land<br>• amber spider fossils found prove they existed more than 30 million years ago |
| PURPOSE (What do they do?) (What are they for?) | • spin webs which catch insects<br>• eat insects<br>• larger spiders also eat frogs<br>• play important part in the ecosystem<br>• catch annoying & harmful insects |
| VENOMOUS | • use venom to kill their prey<br>• venom mostly harmless to humans (& pets)<br>• in Europe exceptions are black widow & water spiders<br>• in Australia many spiders give a nasty bite (e.g. redback spiders) and without anti-venom certain spiders can kill (e.g. funnel-web spider) |
| WEBS | • spin webs of extremely strong silk thread |
| LEGEND, FICTION, FILMS | • Mohammed, Yoritomo, David in the Bible saved by spider's webs hiding them<br>• Robert the Bruce encouraged to carry on his fight by watching a spider spinning a web<br>• Spiderman – comic strip hero who gained incredible strength, sixth sense and ability to scale walls, walk on ceilings – uses his powers to fight evil<br>• Little Miss Muffet – scared by spider<br>• Arachnophobia – horror film based on fear of spiders |

| Title | **Factual report: Spiders** | |
|---|---|---|
| **Classification statement** | My report is about spiders. Spiders belong to the arachnid family. They are not insects. | *What they are*<br>*What they belong to* |
| **Key features** | Many people do not like the way spiders look. They have delicate bodies, eight long legs and can move so quickly that it can be hard to catch them. They can have 2, 4, 6, up to 12 eyes. Many people are scared of spiders and try to squash them or sweep them away. The spiders found in England are harmless, but in other countries like Australia spiders can give a nasty bite. Some can even kill a person if they are not treated quickly for the bite. | *Appearance*<br><br><br><br>*Venom* |
| | There are different types of spider found all over the world. Spiders have been around for millions of years. Fossils have been found which prove this. | *Location – place and time* |
| | Spiders spin webs to catch insects and then they gobble them up. They get rid of insects from houses and gardens and so people should not kill them but be glad they are there. | *Function/purpose* |
| | Many people are afraid of spiders. There are many books and films about spiders that are meant to scare people, such as 'Arachnaphobia'. Even Little Miss Muffet was scared by a spider! | *Books/plays/ poems* |
| **Significance** | Spiders are not dangerous. They are needed to get rid of harmful insects from houses. | *Why spiders are important* |
| **Summary statement** | The spiders found in England do more good than harm and do not deserve their scary reputation. | *Reminder of the main point* |

# SPIDERS

| | | |
|---|---|---|
| *No context – also information not accurate – some spiders will harm you.* | I would like to inform you that spiders are harmless, they will not hurt you at all, however they are very delicate. | *It is written in a very informal style* |
| *Function – what spiders do – spin webs and eat insects in the house* | A good thing about spiders is if you have insects in your house spiders will spin a web and wait for the insects to stick onto the web and the spider will lash out like a cheetah and eat them! | |
| *What spiders eat.* *Repeats function – in the garden* | Spiders do not eat plants and defenetly don't eat grass and don't make it turn into a horrible brown colour and people who say they do are wrong. They get rid of insects in your garden that might damage your plants. | *It is clear from the information in this report that very little research into spiders has been carried out – single point is repeated.* |
| *Repeats function in the context that spiders are 'a good thing'* | People who complain about spiders spinning webs in their house should know that there were probably insects inside their house for example flies, ants and it has probably eaten them up. | *The purpose of the report seems confused – was it to reinstate the reputation of spiders?* |
| *Repeats main point* | Spiders are not dangerous they are HARMLESS and if you would explain it properly to your children that they are not scary and won't bite and tell them they are delicate, harmless and don't hurt you at all. Spiders are more scared of us than we are of them. | *Similarly audience – what is the audience for this report? – people who are afraid of spiders?* *The lack of clarity as to the purpose and audience makes this report repetitious and confused.* |

*Year 5 pupil's report on spiders, before using the SUCCESS Approach*

# SPIDERS

| | | |
|---|---|---|
| ***Classification/ Context Statement*** | My report is about spiders. Spiders belong to the arachnid family. They are not insects. | *The organisation of this report (following the structural model outlined in Success Sheet 1) is much improved.* |
| ***Appearance*** <br><br><br><br><br><br><br><br><br> ***Venomous*** | People don't like the way they look. Spiders have delicate bodies, eight long legs and they move fast so it can be hard to catch them. They can have 2, 4, 6 up to 12 eyes. Many people are scared of spiders and try to squash them or sweep them away. The spiders we have in England are harmless, but in other countries like Australia they can give a nasty bite and some can even kill you if you do not get quick treatment for the bite. | *It has an opening paragraph which provides a context for the report.* <br><br> *There is a logical development of ideas.* <br><br> *And the summary statement neatly rounds off the report.* |
| ***Location*** <br><br><br><br> ***Function Significance*** <br><br><br><br><br><br> ***Fear of spiders*** | There are different types of spider found all over the world. Spiders have been around for millions of years. Fossils have been found that prove it. <br><br> Spiders spin webs to catch insects and then they gobble them up. They get rid of insects from our houses and gardens. So you should not kill them but be glad they are there. <br><br> Lots of people are afraid of spiders and there are books and films about spiders that are meant to scare you. Little Miss Muffet was scared by a spider! | *However, the use of informal language is still present, suggesting that either the teacher did not make sufficiently clear the purpose and audience for the report or the pupil has not yet begun to appreciate the differences between formal and informal language and some further work is required.* |
| ***Summary Statement*** | Spiders are not dangerous and we need them to get rid of harmful insects. They don't deserve their scary reputation. | |

*Year 5 pupil's report on spiders, after using the SUCCESS Approach*

# Exemplar: Information Recording Grid

**Title/subject of report:** My Plant _____

| KEY FEATURES | NOTES |
|---|---|
| CLASSIFICATION<br>Is it a flower or a vegetable? | |
| APPEARANCE<br>What does it look like?<br><br>What size is it?<br><br>What colour is it?<br><br>What smell does it have?<br><br>What can be seen under the lens?<br><br>Stem<br><br>Leaf<br><br>Flower<br><br>Anything else? | |
| LOCATION<br>Where does it grow? | |
| FUNCTION<br>Is it used for anything? | |

Name :- Rebecca Jones          Date :- 11·9·02

L.O. To write a report about the Victorians

## My Report

Queen Victorian had 8 children and she was married to Prinse Albert. When Albert had died Queen victoria wore black. The clothes ladies wore very very long dresses. The men wore very tall hats. The poor children went to work in dangerous places. There were famous people in Victorian times like Florence nightingale, a nurse who wanted better training for nureses and cleaner hospitals. Alexander Graham bell invented the telephone, Joseph swan – invented the electric light bulb.

Good try Rebecca you have included some interesting facts.

*Factual report on the Victorians written by a Year 4 pupil, before using the SUCCESS Approach*

| A report on the Victorians | Title – tells the reader the subject of the report |
|---|---|
| The Victorians were people who lived about a hundred years ago,  They were called after Queen Victoria herself. They lived in the British Isles and Victoria ruled the British Isles. | Contextual paragraph – what they are, who gave them the name, where they lived. |
| The rich women wore long dresses and Bonnets or hats. They wore boots rather than shoes.  The rich men wore top hats with tail coats. The boy's wore knicker bockers, girls wore long frilly dresses that looked pretty with bonnets and their hair in ringlets. However, the poor wore ragged clothes with patches. | Key feature – clothing – distinguishing between rich and poor.<br><br>Linking word |
| The Victorians used horses to pull boats, buses and Tramcars as well as carts, but when steam was invented the horses stopped being used as much but still pulled carts. The penny farthing was a very popular bike but they had two different  sized wheels and were very hard to drive. | Key feature – transport |
| Many inventions changed people's lives, for example the camera, Queen Victoria was the first person to have her picture taken.  The penny black was the very first postage stamp. Electric light were an important discovery.  Before that there were gas lamps and candles. | Key feature – inventions |
| Famous Victorians included Florence Nightingale who was a nures. She helped wouned soldiers in the war, they called her The Lady of the lamp because she had a lamp with her. Charles Dickens was an author. He wrote stories about life in Victorian times. He wrote a story called Oliver Twist and A Christmas Carol. Alexander Graham Bell invented the telephone and Brunel built bridges and railways. | Key feature – famous Victorians |
| Our life today wouldn't be the same without the influence of the Victorian era.  our life today wouldn't be the same without the things that the Victorians invented. The Victorians made our lives better.  In addition sewers were built and museums and many other things. There fore They are (spesh)x special because of what they did to improve our lives today. | Significance of the Victorians<br><br><br>Summary statement reminding the reader of the main point |

*Factual report on the Victorians written by the same Year 4 pupil, after using the SUCCESS Approach*

# COMPARING AND CONTRASTING: THE OSPREY AND THE VULTURE

**When hunger calls, the osprey can catch its prey in one fell swoop ...**

The osprey is found in most parts of the world. Although it is a member of the falcon family, it is sometimes called the "fish-hawk", preying on pike, trout, carp, bream, roach and salmon. The osprey hovers and circles above likely fishing waters. When it spots a fish, it sweeps back its wings and dives downwards. At the last moment it brings its head up, thrusts its talons forward and slows itself down by spreading its wings. Sometimes the osprey goes fully underwater to reach its prey. Then it rises up again, flapping its wings to shake off the spray, with the fish tightly in its talons.

**When hunger calls, a vulture has no need to kill ...**

The vulture here belongs to an Old World species that inhabits the plains of East Africa. A vulture hardly ever kills for food, preferring to eat animals that are dead. Its eyesight is excellent, enabling it to scan the landscape for signs of carrion high in the sky. Once it has discovered food, others will often join it: a large carcass may be attended by fifty birds or more. Vultures are able to digest even long-dead carrion. Although their eating habits may seem repulsive to us, they actually perform a very useful service in clearning away animal remains from the territories they inhabit.

Extracts from *When Hunger Calls* by Bert Kitchen
(Walker Books)

# REPORTS INVOLVING COMPARING/CONTRASTING
## INFORMATION RECORDING GRID (1)

**Title:** The Osprey and the Vulture

| What I am comparing | Osprey | Vulture |
|---|---|---|
| **Classification**<br>What do they belong to? | | |
| **Location**<br>Where do you find them? | | |
| **Function**<br>What do they do?<br><br>What are their prey?<br><br>How do they find their prey?<br><br>What do they do with their prey?<br><br>Do they hunt alone? | | |
| **Purpose**<br>Do they fulfil any purpose beyond feeding themselves? | | |
| **Opinion**<br>What is your opinion of each of them? | | |

# REPORTS INVOLVING COMPARING/CONTRASTING
# INFORMATION RECORDING GRID (2)

**Title:** _The Osprey and the Vulture_

Fill in this table saying what things are similar about the osprey and the vulture and what things you think are different. Use the information you gathered on Information Recording Grid (1) to help you complete this sheet.

| Similarities | Differences |
| --- | --- |
|  |  |
|  |  |
|  |  |
|  |  |
|  |  |
|  |  |

Name Ryan Standring        Date 19.9.02        Year 3
LO:to write a report about the juniors.

## My Report

In the Junior's we have a longer dinner time play. We have no milk or aster noon play. The insants have no team poibts. Juniors get harder work than the insants. The juniors finish school at quarter past 3. The juniors go to suiming and the insants dont. We have hymn books and insants dont. Juniors get lots os home work. When it's sirst play junior's go out when they are ready. We have to put are pumps on and the insants don't. We have dinner besore the insants, Juniors play soot ball on the grass, Sometimes insants do but juniors do mostly. Sometimes insants and juniors aster school goto soot ball clubs, Judo, Franch, club and computer and choir.

Year 3

*Example of Year 3 pupil's report writing, before 'Success' input*

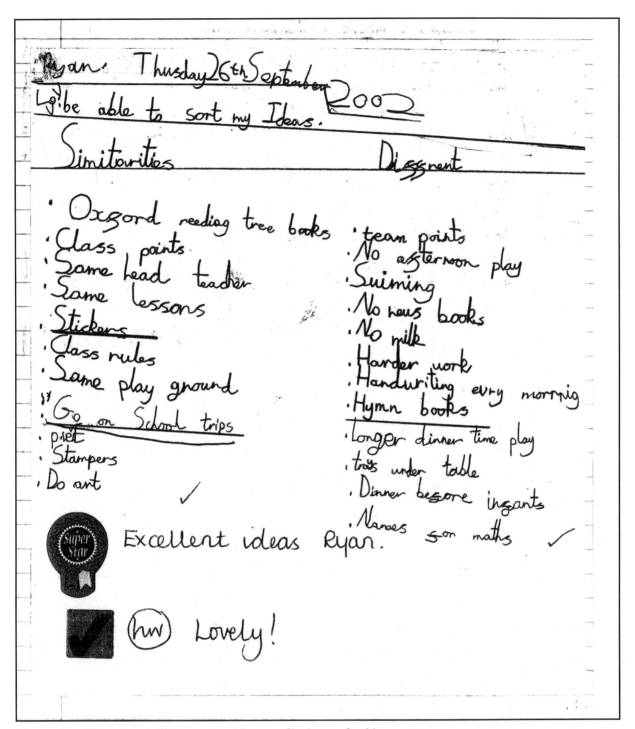

Ryan. Thursday 26th September 2002

L. to be able to sort my Ideas.

Similarities                    Different

- Oxford reading tree books    · team points
- Class points                 · No afternoon play
- Same head teacher            · Suiming
- Same lessons                 · No news books
- Stickers                     · No milk
- Class rules                  · Harder work
- Same play ground             · Handwriting evry morning
- Go on School trips           · Hymn books
- peE                          · Longer dinner time play
- Stampers                     · trays under table
- Do art                       · Dinner before infants
                               · Names for maths  ✓
          ✓

Excellent ideas Ryan.

(hw) Lovely!

*Example of Year 3 pupil's report writing: preliminary drafting*

Ryan Standring.

4   Thursday 3rd October 2002

| Features | Think about! | Examples | |
|---|---|---|---|
| Title | Your title should tell the reader what you are comparing and contrasting. | Life in the Juniors and life in the Infants. | What It's like In the Juniors? |
| Introduction | Tell the reader what you are comparing and contrasting and why. | In this report I will describe differences and similarities between life in the Juniors and life in the Infants, so that the year two children will understand what will change and stay the same when they become juniors. | Hi My report is about the infants and Juniors. It is for the Year 2 children and Juniors. So that the Year 2 can read it. |
| Similarity 1 paragraph | Think about all the key features you are comparing and contrasting and chose those that you think are most important. | A key aspect I wish to describe is ...... | In the juniors we still do tips and total maths. Because we both got to on school |
| Difference 1 paragraph | • Function(what is the juniors/infants) • Location (place/time) • Appearance (what it/they are like) • Purpose (why) | For playtimes, however, the infants have two and have a longer lunchtime while we have to work and get no milk. | In the juniors we have hide hymn books. |
| Similarity 2 paragraph | | Another similarity between life in the infants and life in the juniors is ... | then because they are all juniors sing |
| Difference 2 paragraph | | Furthermore there are differences in the way we are rewarded. In the Juniors we get team points and lunchtime merits. | Another similarity between life in the juniors is that we get stickers in the juniors and good work. In the infants we get stood out Mrs Bob put you in detention. is you see Mrs Whitbread name in the |
| Further similarities/differences paragraphs | THINK! Is there any further information which would grab the reader's attention? | They are also alike/different in that... ...they are comparable in... Moreover... In addition... | The infants and juniors are the same because they both has 0x5nd reading tree bookstill. |
| Summary statement | Have you thought about ALL of the information you have written and told the reader whether your ideas are mainly similar or mainly different? | Although some aspects of life in the Juniors remain the same as in the Infants, even these differ slightly. All of .......are ......but.......are ......better. | Although some things about is different. I think the junior and juniors because people will settle into the really friendly. |

Teacher adapted 'Success' sheet use

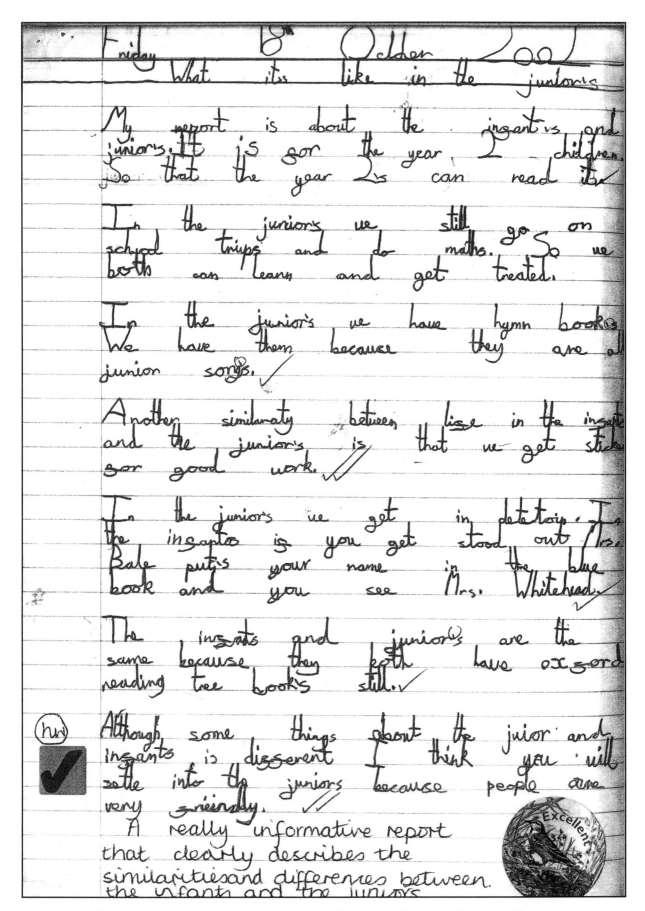

Friday 8th October 2001

What it's like in the juniors

My report is about the infants and juniors. It is for the year 2 children. So that the year 2s can read it.

In the juniors we still go on school trips and do maths. So we both can learn and get treated.

In the junior's we have hymn books. We have them because they are all junior songs. ✓

Another similaraty between lise in the infants and the junior's is that we get stickers for good work. ✓

In the juniors we get in detetoip. In the infants is you get stood out. Mrs Bale puts your name in the blue book and you see Mrs. Whitehead. ✓

The infants and junior's are the same because they both have oxford reading tree books still. ✓

Although some things about the juior and infants is disserent I think you will sofle into the juniors because people are very friendly. ✓✓

A really informative report that clearly describes the similaritiesand differences between the infants and the juniors

*Example of Year 3 pupil's report writing: the finished report, after using 'Success' Sheet*

# SUCCESS SHEET 1: FACTUAL REPORT: *Ideas draft*

| Features | Think about! | Examples | My own examples |
|---|---|---|---|
| *Title* | Your title should tell the reader the subject of your report in no more than four words. | Spiders | |
| *Classification/ Context statement* | Tell the reader:<br>… what they are<br>Tell the reader what they belong to.<br>Don't forget to think about where and when. | Spiders belong to …<br><br>Different species can be found … | |
| *Consider which of these are key features for your subject*<br>*(Add any others which are appropriate)* | Think about all of the key features and write about those that are important to your subject.<br><br>Try to identify additional key features of your subject.<br><br>Add other information which will capture the reader's interest. | (*Appearance – what do they look like?*)<br>– eight legs, have 2, 4, 6 or up to 12 eyes …<br><br>(*Location – where are they found?*)<br>– different species around the world<br><br>(*Purpose- what do they do?*)<br>– spin webs to catch prey<br><br>( – *what are they for?*)<br>– eat harmful insects<br><br>Spiders' venom<br>Spiders' webs<br>Legend/fiction/film | |
| *Significance* | Tell the reader what makes your subject special. | Spiders are an important part of the world's ecosystem because they … | |
| *Summary statement* | End your report with a short reminder of the main points, in different words this time! | Most spiders are harmless to humans and necessary to get rid of annoying and harmful insects. They certainly don't deserve the evil image they are given. | |

# SUCCESS SHEET 2: FACTUAL REPORT: *How well have I done?*

| Features | Have I thought about? | YES/NO | Notes for redrafting |
|---|---|---|---|
| *Title* | Does my title tell the reader the subject of my report in no more than four words? | | |
| *Classification/ Context statement* | Have I told the reader: … what they are? Have I told the reader what they belong to? Have I thought about where and when? | | |
| *Consider the key features* | Have I thought about all of the key features and written about those that are important to my subject? | | |
| *Appearance (what they look like)* *Location (place/time)* *Purpose (what they do, what they are for)* | Have I identified additional key features for my subject? Have I added other information which will capture the reader's interest? | | |
| *Significance* | Have I told the reader what makes my subject special? | | |
| *Summary statement* | Does my report end with a short reminder of the main point? | | |

93

# SUCCESS SHEET 1: REPORT (COMPARING AND CONTRASTING TYPE 1): *Ideas draft*

| Features | Think about! | Examples | My own examples |
|---|---|---|---|
| *Title* | Your title should tell the reader what you are comparing and contrasting. | Comparing ... my home town of Bletchley with Ilam in Derbyshire | |
| *Opening paragraph/ Context statement* | Tell the reader what you are comparing and contrasting and why. | In this report I will compare and contrast ... in order to understand which are the same and which are different. | |
| *Similarity 1*<br><br><br><br><br>*Difference 1* | Think about the aspects you have identified to compare and contrast and select the most important to your subject<br>• Appearance<br>•<br>•<br>•<br>• | Both Bletchley and Ilam are ...<br><br>In appearance they ...<br><br>They are similar in that they ...<br><br>Another similarity is ...<br><br>The main difference is (in Bletchley) there is ..., while (in Ilam) ... | |
| *Similarity 2*<br><br><br>*Difference 2* | Select the next aspect you want to compare and contrast.<br>• work | They are also alike/different in that ...<br><br>They are similar in that ... | |
| *Further paragraphs outlining similarities and differences* | Select the other aspects you want to compare and contrast.<br>• traffic<br>• leisure | There are other similarities/differences ...<br><br>Another important similarity/difference is ... | |
| *Summary statement* | Consider ALL the information you have written and then tell the reader whether the two things are mainly similar or mainly different. | Although some aspects of ... are similar to ..., for the most part they are very different ..., because one is ... and the other is ... | |

94

# SUCCESS SHEET 2: REPORT (COMPARING AND CONTRASTING TYPE 1): *How well have I done?*

| Features | Have I thought about? | YES/NO | Notes for redrafting |
|---|---|---|---|
| *Title* | Have I told the reader what I am comparing and contrasting? | | |
| *Opening paragraph/ Context statement* | Have I told the reader what I am comparing and contrasting and why? | | |
| *Similarity 1* | Have I picked the most important things to compare? Which have I selected first? | | |
| *Difference 1* | Have I told the reader the similarities and differences in the first aspect I chose to compare and contrast? | | |
| *Similarity 2* | What was the second aspect I wanted to compare and contrast? | | |
| *Difference 2* | Have I told the reader what the similarities and differences are? | | |
| *Further paragraphs outlining similarities and differences* | Which other aspect(s) have I selected to compare and contrast? Have I told the reader the similarities and differences? | | |
| *Summary statement* | Have I summed up and told the reader what the most important similarities and differences are? | | |

# SUCCESS SHEET 1: REPORT (COMPARING AND CONTRASTING TYPE 2): *Ideas draft*

| Features | Think about! | Examples | My own examples |
|---|---|---|---|
| Title | Your title should tell the reader what you are comparing and contrasting. | Life in Victorian times compared with life today | |
| Opening paragraph/ Context statement | Tell the reader what you are comparing and contrasting and why. | In this report I will compare and contrast life in Victorian times and life today, in order to understand what has changed and what has stayed the same. | |
| Similarity 1 | Think about the aspects you have identified to compare and contrast. Select those aspects which are similar. | A key aspect I wish to consider is … | |
| Similarity 2 | | Another similarity is … | |
| Further similarites | • <br> • <br> • <br> • | They are also alike in that … <br> Moreover … <br> In addition … <br> … whereas … | |
| Difference 1 | Now select the aspects which are different | A major difference is … | |
| Difference 2 | | Another difference is … | |
| Further differences | • <br> • <br> • <br> • | They are also different in that … <br> A further difference is … <br> Additionally … | |
| Summary statement | Sum up: what are the most important things that have changed? What things have not changed? | Although some aspects of life today, such as … remain the same as in Victorian times, the main changes are … | |

# SUCCESS SHEET 2: REPORT (COMPARING AND CONTRASTING TYPE 2): *How well have I done?*

| Features | Have I thought about? | YES/NO | Notes for redrafting |
|---|---|---|---|
| *Title* | Have I told the reader what I am comparing and contrasting? | | |
| *Opening paragraph/ Context statement* | Have I told the reader what I am comparing and contrasting and why? | | |
| *Similarity 1* | Have I selected a number of aspects which are similar? | | |
| *New sentence Similarity 2* | Have I made clear what is similar for each aspect? | | |
| *Further similarites* | | | |
| *Difference 1* | Have I selected a number of aspects which are different? | | |
| *Difference 2* | Have I made it clear what is different for each aspect? | | |
| *Further differences* | | | |
| *Summary statement* | Does my final paragraph tell the reader whether the aspects are mainly similar or mainly different? | | |

# SUCCESS SHEET 1: REPORT (COMPARING AND CONTRASTING TYPE 3): *Ideas draft*

| Features | Think about! | Examples | My own examples |
|---|---|---|---|
| *Title* | Your title should tell the reader what you are comparing and contrasting. | Comparing the weather in England and the Arctic | |
| *Opening paragraph/ Context statement* | Tell the reader what you are comparing and contrasting and why. | I want to compare the weather in England and the Arctic to see if it is mainly similar or mainly different. | |
| *Paragraph comparing first aspect in both subjects* | Tell the reader both the similarities and the differences in this aspect for both subjects of the report, e.g. the weather for both places in summer. | In summer … <br> The weather is often alike in that … <br> But unlike in that … | |
| *Paragraph comparing second aspect in both subjects* | Tell the reader both the similarities and the differences in this aspect for both subjects of the report. eg the weather for both places in autumn. | In autumn … <br> They are also similar in … <br> They are different, however, in … | |
| *Paragraph comparing third aspect in both subjects* | Tell the reader both the similarities and the differences in this aspect for both subjects of the report. eg the weather for both places in winter. | In winter … <br> (this aspect) is the same … <br> While (this aspect) is different … | |
| *Paragraph comparing fourth aspect in both subjects* | Tell the reader both the similarities and the differences in this aspect for both subjects of the report. eg the weather for both places in spring. | In spring too/also <br> This is the same … <br> But this is different … | |
| *Summary statement* | Consider ALL the information you have written and then tell the reader whether the aspects are mainly similar or mainly different. | There are some similarities in the weather patterns of both England and the Arctic. This is because … The main difference is the temperature. It is much colder in the Arctic because … | |

# SUCCESS SHEET 2: REPORT (COMPARING AND CONTRASTING TYPE 3): *How well have I done?*

| Features | Have I thought about? | YES/NO | Notes for redrafting |
|---|---|---|---|
| *Title* | Does my title tell the reader what I am comparing and contrasting? | | |
| *Opening paragraph/ Context statement* | Have I told the reader what I am comparing and contrasting and why? | | |
| *Paragraph comparing first aspect in both subjects* | Have I told the reader both the similarities and the differences in my first aspect for both subjects of the report? | | |
| *Paragraph comparing second aspect in both subjects* | Have I told the reader both the similarities and the differences in my second aspect for both subjects? | | |
| *Paragraph comparing third aspect in both subjects* | Have I told the reader both the similarities and the differences in my third aspect for both subjects? | | |
| *Paragraph comparing fourth aspect in both subjects* | Have I told the reader both the similarities and the differences in my fourth aspect for both subjects? | | |
| *Paragraph comparing other aspect in both subjects* | Have I told the reader both the similarities and the differences in any other aspect(s) for both subjects? | | |
| *Summary statement* | Have I considered ALL the information I've written and told the reader whether the aspects are mainly similar or mainly different? | | |

# 5 Writing newspaper reports

## 1 Definition

Newspaper reports provide information about a single event or a series of events. Their purpose is to inform their readers about events or issues which are of interest. A key feature of newspaper reports is their use of attention-grabbing headlines to attract readers to the article. A major difference from other forms of report is the layout, with information presented in columns.

## 2 NLS Framework links

### Year 3 Term 3
- **T22** 'experiment with recounting the same event in a variety of ways, e.g. in the form of a story, a letter, a news report'

### Year 6 Term 1
- **T15** 'to develop a journalistic style through considering:
    - balanced and ethical reporting;
    - what is of public interest in events;
    - the interest of the reader;
    - selection and presentation of information'
- **T16** 'to use the styles and conventions of journalism to report on e.g. real or imaginary events'
- **T18** 'to use IT to plan, revise, edit writing to improve accuracy and conciseness and to bring it to publication standard, e.g. through compiling a class newspaper, paying attention to accuracy, layout and presentation'

## 3 Text level features (purpose and organisation)

*Organisation*
Most newspaper reports are organised as follows:
- Headline
- By-line
- Lead Paragraph
- Body
- Sources
- Illustration and Caption

## 4 Sentence level features (style, punctuation and grammar)

*Style*
- use of frequent short paragraphs (usually no more than two sentences)
- use of short sentences

- information factual and to the point
- consistent use of the third person
- conscious use of tense changes for effect
- quotation of/use of sources to add detail
- manipulation of detail to sustain reader interest
- sometimes use of emotive language to provoke reader response

*Punctuation*
- use of frequent short paragraphs
- use of exclamation marks to add emphasis (usually in headlines)
- use of direct speech to quote sources
- use of commas to separate clauses in extended sentences
- use of commas, brackets, dashes to indicate parenthesis

*Grammar*
- effective use of both direct and reported speech
- use of ellipsis in order to condense information e.g. 'loading' one sentence with a broad range of information detail

## 5 Word level features

*Vocabulary*
- use of broad range of causal connectives e.g. *consequently, subsequently*
- use of emotive language in tabloid reporting

*Spelling*
- event-specific language
- emotive language e.g. *outrageous, horrified, charming, delightful*

## 6 Newpaper reports and note-making

Writing newspaper reports can involve recounting events, explaining events or phenomena, reporting what has happened or what people have said, or discussing important issues of current interest – all presented in a style appropriate to the specific newspaper's target readership. Thus the note-making techniques outlined in the chapters on writing recounts (timelines), explanations (flow charts), reports (spider diagrams and information grids), discussion (for and against information grids) may be relevant to specific newspaper writing tasks, and teachers should provide guidance or models where appropriate. A note-making format is included in this chapter (spider diagram, page 111) and can be used both for making notes for articles to be written and for making notes from existing articles. Success Sheet 1 (page 117), which outlines the basic structure of a newspaper article, also provides an effective note-making format for newspaper articles.

Using pictures with captions, annotated diagrams and maps to illustrate the text are important note-making techniques and, as they are also features of many newspaper articles, these should be covered in Year 3 and re-enforced each time pupils write newspaper articles.

## 7 Teachers' notes

Journalistic writing is best examined through existing newspaper articles, but the wider curriculum can provide ideas for writing newspaper articles, e.g.

- in history – articles about historical events, using a 'you are there' approach
- in geography – environmental issues such as flooding or drought.

However, the main source for writing newspaper articles is likely to be reporting school events, such as productions or concerts. Fiction currently being read with the class may also provide ideas and stimulus for writing articles.

Newspaper article writing can, at worst, be little more than a story in columns with an added headline above and a picture at its base. If this situation is to be improved then pupils must become familiar with the sequential features of newspaper article writing  i.e. headline, by-line, lead paragraph, body, illustration and caption.

It is also necessary that pupils become familiar with journalistic writing. In order to do this a wide range of newspaper articles should be used and discussed in the classroom. Features of 'newspaper language' which the teacher may wish to discuss/ explore with pupils include:

- formal newspaper language (avoidance of first person pronoun)
- journalistic conventions e.g. name followed by age of person included in article
- pertinent information-loaded sentences (avoidance of irrelevant details)
- use of sources to enhance the report and/or create an empathic response.

The more pupils read newspaper reports, the better their own writing will become with regard to text organisation. Newspaper reports, however, are enormously fluid and varied. We have provided an example (page 107) which can be deconstructed with the class. Teachers may prefer to use a more current news story of interest to the pupils for deconstruction.

An example of a newspaper report by a child, written after the lesson using the SUCCESS Approach, is included on page 104.

*Recommended sequence of lessons*

1 Deconstruction of an existing newspaper article (Activity 1).

2 Teacher models how to use Success Sheet 1 to make notes for a newspaper article.

3 Shared writing session, demonstrating how to use the notes on Success Sheet 1 and focussing on key points highlighted during the deconstruction activity.

4 Pupils make notes for their article using the appropriate Success Sheet 1.

5 Pupils plan and write their first draft.

6 Pupils evaluate their newspaper article using the appropriate Success Sheet 2.

7 Teacher provides feedback to pupils on their articles and evaluations – this can be done orally or in writing, as appropriate to the age/stage of development of their pupils.

8 Teacher summarises what has been learned about this text form with class.

Additional activities are provided to meet the different objectives for Years 3 and 6 (see NLS links, page 100) and should be used after the above sequence of lessons.

Activity 2 is appropriate for pupils in Year 3, and is designed to meet objective T22, 'recounting the same event in a variety of ways.'

Activities 3 and 4 are aimed at pupils in Year 6. These are designed to meet objective T15, 'to develop a journalistic style'.

# Spaceship at Quiet School!

A Spaceship has landed in a quiet school in Herefordshire! ~~By~~ Reports stephen Watkins.

There was a crowd of pupils and teachers all staring at a spaceship in the middle of the playing fields. ~~The~~ It happened on Friday 13th.

The door of the spaceship opened slowly but ~~and~~ steadily and mist came pouring out and all you could see ~~was~~ a shadow. The alien stepped into the light and everybody gasped. There was nothing more unhuman. It was: 5 foot, green, 2 antenni's webbed feet and a whithered look.

The alien said in a crackle "We ~~weel~~ want ~~at~~ a young boy and girl for (t) my heir." A boy and girl walked reuctlly to ~~him~~, he turned and ~~the~~ children ~~followed~~ the alien Everyone

began to weep in an adult manner as if somebo~~dy~~ important had just died. The spaceship took off and was staring up at the sky wondering will we ever see them again.

If you have got a story Fax: 01981 240465 and email is: Watkis@ watkins.screaming.net.

*A newspaper report written after only one lesson using the SUCCESS Approach (courtesy of Ewyas Harold School, Herefordshire)*

# 8 Activity suggestions

*Activity 1: Deconstructing a newspaper report*

Pupils are given a copy of the newspaper article 'Suspension for teacher accused of tying pupil to a chair' as a stimulus for discussion (pages 107–8). The article conforms to the structural model used in the sheets included within this chapter and provides a useful starting point for the investigation of newspaper reports and the subsequent development of the pupils' own journalistic style. This article is suitable for pupils in Year 6. A simpler newspaper article, 'Rock star's Shoplifting Shame' (pages 109–10) which also conforms to the model is provided as an option for this activity and this article may be more appropriate for pupils in Year 3.

The teacher then leads a discussion session to highlight the ways in which the journalist has made each feature effective:
- the headline
- person's name on the by-line
- who? what? when? why? and how? are all covered in the lead paragraph
- details are added in the body of the article
- direct and reported speech are used when quoting sources
- possible reasons for the lack of a photograph and caption could be discussed.

Optional sheets for making notes before pupils write their own newspaper articles are also provided (pages 111–12).

*Activity 2: Recounting the same event in a variety of ways*

The same newspaper articles could be used to provide opportunities for pupils recounting the same event in a variety of ways. The pupils could be asked to write the events described in the first article as a narrative from the point of view of either another pupil, the teacher or the pupil involved. Or they could be asked imagine they had been a pupil in the class at the time of the incident in order to write a letter telling a friend what had happened in class that day.

Alternatively events from history (such as a Viking raid on a village, the Fire of London, Sir Francis Drake and the Armada, or the Blitz) can be used as the stimulus for recounting the same event as a story, in a letter or in a newspaper article.

In Year 3 another source of events which can be recounted in a variety of ways is to be found in the stories which pupils read. There are excellent sources to be found in the range of myths, legends, fables and traditional stories read in Term 2 or the adventure and mystery stories read in Term 3.

Real events which happen in the school or the local area can also be successfully exploited to stimulate writing about an event in a variety of ways.

Pupils in Year 6 should also write newspaper reports 'using the styles and conventions of journalism to report on real or imaginary events' (Term 1 T16). Consequently teachers of Year 6 pupils should also exploit the opportunities provided by school, local or international events as stimulus for writing newspaper reports. Similarly events in the novels, plays and stories they read can provide the 'story' for a newspaper report. The main difference for Year 6 pupils would be in the fact that the reports they produce should reflect the objectives outlined in Term 1 T15.

*Activity 3: Comparing and contrasting newspaper reports of the same event*

With older pupils a comparison of tabloid and broadsheet styles will deepen their understanding of journalistic style and language – looking at the treatment of the same story in both tabloid and broadsheet can be a useful activity in this respect. Two articles about an earthquake taken from the *Daily Express* and the *Guardian* on 27 September 2003 are provided (see page 113) to support this activity, but teachers may wish to find other appropriate and more topical reports for their classes.

A useful way to begin this activity is by comparing the information that has been included in each report. A grid is provided for this activity (page 114).

The key points for discussion are:
• looking at the information grid, what is the significance of any differences in the information provided/not provided?
• the use of pictures and captions in the tabloid version
• headlines – vocabulary choices, size
• style of language used in both articles – emotive or formal?

The discussion should be framed by consideration of the objectives for Year 6 Term 1 (page 100).

*Activity 4: Writing in tabloid/broadsheet style*

Once again the objectives outlined in Year 6 Term 1 T15 will frame this activity. Pupils are given *either* a broadsheet version *or* a tabloid version of a newspaper report and their task is to write the same story for the other form of newspaper.

A pair of articles is provided for this activity (pages 115–16), or teachers may provide their own, more up to date examples.

# Suspension for teacher accused of tying pupil to a chair

A teacher who allegedly tied a disruptive primary school pupil to his chair with a skipping rope has been suspended, it emerged yesterday.

Mabel Tanner, a supply teacher, was suspended by the LEA after being accused of strapping an eight year old to his seat in an attempt to stop him wandering around the classroom.

Parents said Mrs Tanner first verbally disciplined the boy for disrupting her class and continually walking round the room.

When that failed, and the boy got out of his chair again, she asked him if she needed to tie him to his chair to make him sit in it. The boy got up again, and Mrs Tanner asked the teaching assistant to go to the gym to get a skipping rope.

As the pupils in Year 4 looked on, Mrs Tanner allegedly tied the boy to his chair.

It is understood he was not tied tightly to the chair and could have freed himself at any time.

But he was freed when the headteacher, Eileen Smith, walked in on the lesson and took the boy away.

Mrs Smith informed the child's father of the incident. The father subsequently made a formal complaint, and the matter was reported to LEA officers.

The LEA has launched an investigation into the incident and Mrs Tanner will learn if she is to be disciplined next week.

It is understood Mrs Tanner has been teaching for 40 years and has an unblemished record.

She had been teaching on supply at the primary school for more than a week when the incident happened.

The boy's father said he had been speaking to his lawyers regarding the incident.

A spokesman for the LEA said: 'We can confirm that a member of supply teaching staff has been suspended while an investigation is underway. At present it is not a disciplinary matter.'

(adapted from an article which appeared in the *Guardian*, 21 March 2003. Names have been changed)

*Headline*

*By-line*

*Lead paragraph*

*Body*
*(the remaining 14 paragraphs making up the story)*

*Sources*

# Suspension for teacher accused of tying pupil to a chair

A teacher who allegedly tied a disruptive primary school pupil to his chair with a skipping rope has been suspended, it emerged yesterday.

Mabel Tanner, a supply teacher, was suspended by the LEA after being accused of strapping an eight year old to his seat in an attempt to stop him wandering around the classroom.

Parents said Mrs Tanner first verbally disciplined the boy for disrupting her class and continually walking round the room.

When that failed, and the boy got out of his chair again, she asked him if she needed to tie him to his chair to make him sit in it. The boy got up again, and Mrs Tanner asked the teaching assistant to go to the gym to get a skipping rope.

As the pupils in Year 4 looked on, Mrs Tanner allegedly tied the boy to his chair.

It is understood he was not tied tightly to the chair and could have freed himself at any time.

But he was freed when the headteacher, Eileen Smith, walked in on the lesson and took the boy away.

Mrs Smith informed the child's father of the incident. The father subsequently made a formal complaint, and the matter was reported to LEA officers.

The LEA has launched an investigation into the incident and Mrs Tanner will learn if she is to be disciplined next week.

It is understood Mrs Tanner has been teaching for 40 years and has an unblemished record.

She had been teaching on supply at the primary school for more than a week when the incident happened.

The boy's father said he had been speaking to his lawyers regarding the incident.

A spokesman for the LEA said: 'We can confirm that a member of supply teaching staff has been suspended while an investigation is underway. At present it is not a disciplinary matter.'

*Note the broad range of information in this opening sentence.*

*Why is the word 'allegedly' used in the first paragraph?*

**Note:**

- *the use of commas to separate clauses in extended sentences*

- *the expanded details in the body of the story*

- *the order of priority the journalist has given to the various details – how has the information been organised?*

- *the use of sources – the names or titles of people who provided the information*

- *the consistent use of the third person throughout*

- *the use of both direct and reported speech*

- *where emotive language is used – 'unblemished' 'disruptive' – what effect does it have? Are there other emotive words you have noticed?*

- *the linking words and phrases used*

# Rock Star's
## Shoplifting Shame!

Aziz Seth, *Crime Correspondent*

Ageing rock star, Gary Beast, was arrested in Brighton yesterday for shoplifting. He was caught red-handed on camera in a well-known Department store.

This is Gary Beast's third arrest for shoplifting in the past two years. His band, 'Bad Breath', split up in 1996 and, since then, Gary has made four failed attempts at comeback. He has fallen on hard times and this may explain his recent behaviour.

The arresting officer explained that Gary had been spotted behaving in a suspicious manner.

When arrested, Gary said tearfully, 'I don't know what came over me.'

The singer will appear before a jury in three week's time.

| | | |
|---|---|---|
| *HEADLINE* | # Rock Star's Shoplifting Shame! | |
| *By-line* | Aziz Seth, *Crime Correspondent* | |
| *Lead paragraph* | Ageing rock star, Gary Beast, was arrested in Brighton yesterday for shoplifting. He was caught red-handed on camera in a well-known Department store. | *Who? – Gary Beast*<br>*What? – arrested*<br>*Where? – department store in Brighton*<br>*Why? – shoplifting*<br>*How? – CCTV* |
| *Body* | This is Gary Beast's third arrest for shoplifting in the past two years. His band, 'Bad Breath', split up in 1996 and, since then, Gary has made four failed attempts at comeback. He has fallen on hard times and this may explain his recent behaviour. | *Background information*<br><br><br><br><br>*Possible explanation* |
| *Sources* | The arresting officer explained that Gary had been spotted behaving in a suspicious manner. | *Source – police officer*<br>*More detail (reported speech)* |
| | When arrested, Gary said tearfully, 'I don't know what came over me.' | *Detail – what he said (direct speech)* |
| | The singer will appear before a jury in three week's time. | *Outcome* |

# Newspaper article: Notes (1)

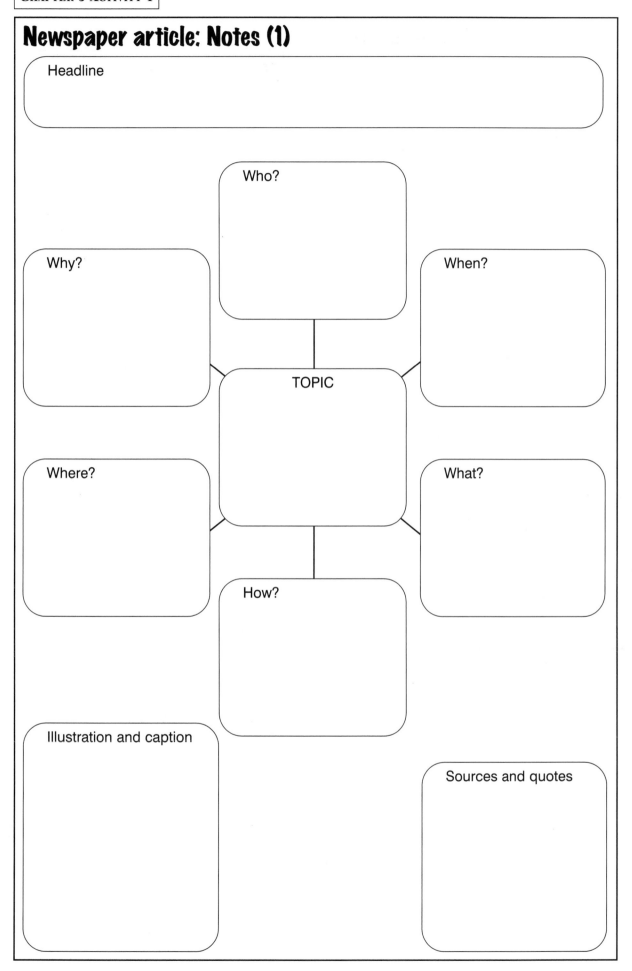

Headline

Who?

Why?

When?

TOPIC

Where?

What?

How?

Illustration and caption

Sources and quotes

# Newspaper article: Notes (2)

| ALL THE Ws | SOURCES | ADDITIONAL DETAIL/QUOTES |
|---|---|---|
| **WHO**<br>is the article about? | | |
| **WHAT**<br>happened? | | |
| **WHERE**<br>did it happen? | | |
| **WHEN**<br>did it happen? | | |
| **HOW**<br>did it happen? | | |
| **WHY**<br>did it happen? | | |

## Japan rocked by undersea tremor

# Quake

A massive earthquake flattened buildings and sank ships when it struck northern Japan yesterday. But only one man died as hundreds were injured after tremors rocked the island of Hokkaido.

Roads were buckled, buildings toppled and oil tanks exploded into flames. The island's airport was closed when its terminal roof collapsed. The quake – measuring 8.0 on the Richter scale – began 26 miles beneath the Pacific, creating huge seas. It was felt as far as Tokyo, 600 miles away. More than 40,000 fled their homes during the aftershocks.

Hokkaido – site of the 1972 Winter Olympics – could be hit by tremors and tidal waves for the next 10 days, weather experts have warned.

*Daily Express*, 27 September 2003

# Hundreds hurt in Japanese quakes

**Justin McCurry** in Osaka

More than 400 people were injured, at least 18 seriously, when two powerful earthquakes struck the island of Hokkaido in northern Japan early yesterday.

The first, measuring 8.0 on the Richter scale, was the strongest felt anywhere in the world this year. It left 16,000 homes without electricity and started a fire at an oil refinery.

Air, land and sea transport was paralysed for most of the day in many parts of the island, which is about 500 miles north of Tokyo. More than 40,000 people were forced to leave their homes by a warning of a tsunami – huge waves – and aftershocks. The tsunami warning was later downgraded.

The authorities asked for troops to be mobilised to distribute fresh water.

The first earthquake struck at 4.50am, and was followed by a slightly less powerful one just after 6am. Cracks appeared in buildings and roads, but no sign of damage was found at any of the island's nuclear power stations.

The city of Kushiro bore the brunt of the quakes. Thirty two flights were cancelled at the airport after the control tower's ceiling collapsed.

The meteorological agency said that at least 24 smaller tremors had been felt by early yesterday evening, and strong aftershocks could continue for the next 10 days.

There was an indirect fatality: a 61 year old man was struck and killed by a car as he was clearing up bottles that had fallen on to the road.

The government promised financial help for the victims.

*Guardian*, 27 September 2003

## Comparing articles on an earthquake in Japan from the *Daily Express* and the *Guardian*

| Information in both | Information only in the *Guardian* | Information only in the *Daily Express* |
|---|---|---|
|  |  |  |

# Charles 'furious' over media frenzy

## Harry's trip to Oz could come to an early end

Prince Harry was last night preparing to quit his gap-year trip to Australia after coming under seige from snoopers.

Palace aides insist it will be impossible for him to continue his three-month visit if Australian paparazzi and media organisations do not leave him alone.

Prince Charles is said to be furious at the intrusion. A St. James Palace source said yesterday: "If things don't change, he'll be on his way home."

Harry, 19, has been working as a £100-a-week jackeroo, or cowboy, at a remote cattle station in the outback.

But within hours of arriving, photographers took up positions around the ranch's massive perimeter.

Helicopters have been buzzing around overhead and a picture of Harry hard at work has already been published in a Brisbane newspaper.

Officials are disappointed their requests for Harry to be left in peace had been ignored. On Thursday the situation had become so grave that Charles's press secretary issued a statement to the Australian media. It said: "We would be pleased if camera crews and photographers at the cattle station would withdraw accordingly."

*Daily Express*, 27 September 2003

# Media may drive Harry home early

**From Roger Maynard** in Sydney

Four days after Prince Harry arrived in Australia for a three month Outback experience as a jackaroo, Buckingham Palace has hinted that it might bring him home early because of the intense level of media interest.

Harry has been beseiged by Australian and British media since he arrived in the remote Queensland cattle property of Tooloombilla, 360 miles west of Brisbane, on Tuesday.

The 40,000 acre farm, co-owned by Annie Hill, a friend of Diana, Princess of Wales, has been staked out by TV and newspaper crews for the past four days, much to the annoyance of the Prince's minders.

Last night, Colleen Harris, press secretary to the Prince of Wales, issued a veiled threat that unless Harry was left alone, the rest of his Australian visit might be in jeopardy.

Ms Harris told *The Times*: "He's gone to the Outback to acquire new trades and have new experiences, but if he's hindered by the media and it's disruptive to his work on the farm, then we will have to look at the options."

Asked if this could mean he would be forced to return home prematurely, she replied: "It's not at that stage yet but it's a plea to the media to give him a bit of space." The Palace's stance was backed by local residents who believe the security surrounding Harry will prevent him from appreciating the true life of the jackaroo.

"It's a real shame if he can't get the chance to enjoy a real Outback experience," one farm worker said.

Ms Harris was more blunt: "Learning about the farm and the jackaroo trade, that's what he wants to do, not dodge the cameras. He can only do this if he's allowed to live peacefully and in privacy away from the media's spotlight."

Prince Harry's new neighbours are bemused by all the fuss. Drinkers at the nearest pub, the Injune Hotel, more than 30 miles away from Tooloombilla, said they were not impressed by the royal visitor. John MacEwan, a publican said: "We're pretty laid back here, except for all the helicopters and the people coming in."

Harry flew into Australia on Tuesday and immediately impressed Australians with his easygoing manner during a photo call at Taronga Zoo in Sydney.

*The Times*, 27 September 2003

# SUCCESS SHEET 1: NEWSPAPER ARTICLE: *Ideas draft*

| Features | Think about! | Example | My own examples |
|---|---|---|---|
| *Headline* | Try to use no more than seven words and include the main point. | Rock Star's shoplifting shame<br>Hunt protestors highlight horror of killing<br>Recipes for disaster (junk food article) | |
| *By-line* | Your name, title, location if the story is world news. | Aziz Seth<br>Defence Correspondent<br>Baghdad | |
| *Lead Paragraph* | Include all the Ws (Who? What? Where? When? Why? – and maybe a How?) in no more than three sentences. | *Who? Gary Beast*<br>*What? was arrested*<br>*Where? in Brighton*<br>*When? yesterday*<br>*Why? for shoplifting.*<br>*How? CCTV* | |
| *Body* | Provide more details about each of the Ws – remember one or two of the Ws will be more important or relevant than others.<br>Write short paragraphs - no more than two or three sentences.<br>Present the information in a balanced and factual way.<br>Keep in mind who will be reading your article as you select and present your information | This is Gary's third arrest for shoplifting in the past two years.<br>His band, Bad Breath, split up in 1992. Since then Gary has had four failed attempts at making a comeback.  He has fallen on hard times and this may explain his recent behaviour. | |
| *Sources* | Include the names or titles of the people who provided the information used in your article.<br>Use both direct and reported speech when quoting what was said. | **(Reported speech)** *The arresting officer explained that Gary had been spotted behaving in a suspicious manner.*<br>**(Direct speech)** *When arrested Gary said tearfully: "I don't know what came over me."* | |
| *Illustration and Caption* | Draw a box where the illustration will be placed and write a brief description of what will appear inside the box.<br>Add a brief caption beneath the box. | **(Description)** *Photograph of Gary Beast being bundled into police van*<br>**(Caption)** *Popstar Gary Beast is led away by police* | |

# SUCCESS SHEET 2: NEWSPAPER ARTICLE: *How well have I done?*

| Features | Have I thought about? | YES/NO | Notes for redrafting |
|---|---|---|---|
| *Headline* | Have I used no more than seven words? Does my headline include the main point? | | |
| *By-line* | Have I included my by-line – my name, my title, the city I am reporting from, if my article is world news? | | |
| *Lead Paragraph* | Have I included all the Ws (Who? What? Where? When? Why? – and maybe a How?) Have I used no more than three sentences? | | |
| *Body* | Have I provided more details about each of the Ws? Which Ws are more important or relevant? Have I written in short paragraphs – no more than two or three sentences in each? Have I presented the information in a balanced and factual way? Have I taken into account who will be reading my article in my selection and presentation of information? | | |
| *Sources* | Have I included the names or titles of the people who provided the information used in my article? Have I used both direct and reported speech when quoting what was said? | | |
| *Illustration and Caption* | Have I indicated where an illustration and caption will be placed? Have I indicated what these are? | | |

118

# 6 Persuasive writing

## 1 Definition

Persuasive writing is composed of structured arguments for or against a specific point of view. The main aim of any persuasive text is to encourage the reader to agree with the writer's point of view. This may be achieved through a combination of explaining, analysing and informing the reader of details pertaining to the writer's particular viewpoint. Persuasive writing is used in many contexts, including essays, books, music, film and television reviews; and letters.

## 2 NLS Framework links

### Year 4 Term 3

- **T21** 'to assemble and sequence points in order to plan the presentation of a point of view, e.g. hunting, school rules'
- **T22** 'to use writing frames if necessary to back up points of view with illustrations and examples'
- **T23** 'to present a point of view in writing, e.g. in the form of a letter, a report or a script, linking points persuasively and selecting style and vocabulary appropriate to the reader'
- **T25** 'to design an advertisement, such as a poster or radio jingle, on paper or screen, e.g. for a school fête or an imaginary product, making use of linguistic and other features learnt from reading examples'

### Year 5 Term 3

- **T17** 'to draft and write individual, group or class letters for real purposes, e.g. put a point of view, comment on an emotive issue, protest; to edit and present to finished state'
- **T18** 'to write a commentary on an issue on paper or screen, (e.g. as a news editorial, leaflet) setting out and justifying a personal view; to use structures from reading to set out and link points, e.g. numbered lists, bullet points'
- **T19** 'to construct an argument in note form or full text to persuade others of a point of view and:
  - present the case to the class or a group
  - evaluate its effectiveness'

### Year 6 Term 2

- **T18** 'to construct effective arguments:
  - developing a point of view logically and effectively;
  - supporting and illustrating points persuasively;
  - anticipating possible objections;

– harnessing the known views, interests and feelings of the audience;

– tailoring the writing to formal presentation where appropriate'

## 3 Text level features (purpose and organisation)

*Organisation*

We suggest the following organisation for persuasive essays:
- Title
- Statement of the writer's viewpoint
- Series of supporting arguments for this viewpoint
- Recognition of alternative viewpoint(s)
- Counter arguments (arguments against the alternative viewpoints)
- Reiteration of original viewpoint (in different words)

## 4 Sentence level features (style, punctuation and grammar)

*Style*
- use of bullet points, numbering to emphasise points, particularly in concluding paragraph
- use of succinct, sharply focused sentences

*Punctuation*
- use of paragraphs to separate each element of the essay
- correct use of commas within sentences to separate phrases or clauses

*Grammar*
- consistent use of timeless present tense e.g. *I strongly believe that ...*

## 5 Word level features (vocabulary and spelling)

*Vocabulary*
- use of broad range of causal connectives e.g. *therefore, furthermore*
- use of appropriate technical vocabulary to support viewpoint
- use of words and phrases to link to alternative viewpoint, e.g. *on the other hand, alternatively, conversely*
- reference to generalised human agents, e.g. *dog breeders, motorbike owners, mountaineers*
- reference to groups (described as nouns) e.g. *the poor, the rich, the elite, the oppressed*

*Spelling*
- use of subject-specific words
- *moreover, furthermore, additionally*

## 6 Note-making and persuasive writing

Persuasive texts come in many forms, such as advertisements, leaflets, letters, reviews and essays. In presentation terms this means a wide range of text forms from advertising copy (where much of the impact is visual and based on illustrations, graphics, layout and colour) through to carefully argued essays outlining a point of view. It is, therefore, important to highlight a range of note-making techniques when dealing with different forms of persuasive text. Keywords remain central to any note-making and are used in advertising copy, where the text is necessarily brief. Keywords set out as bullet points, which are then extended by additional details or examples, are an appropriate note-making technique to demonstrate to pupils for gathering information and ideas for persuasive writing. e.g. making notes for a leaflet to persuade people of the need for a by-pass, the keywords/phrases might be:

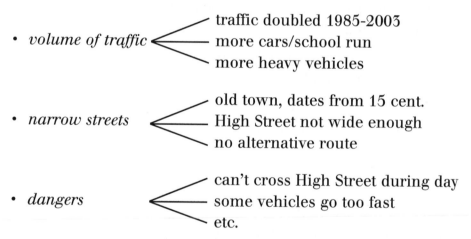

- *volume of traffic*
  - traffic doubled 1985–2003
  - more cars/school run
  - more heavy vehicles

- *narrow streets*
  - old town, dates from 15 cent.
  - High Street not wide enough
  - no alternative route

- *dangers*
  - can't cross High Street during day
  - some vehicles go too fast
  - etc.

A spider diagram is also useful for brainstorming and organising information or ideas (see Activity 2). We would also recommend the use of an information recording grid to organise ideas, where appropriate, before writing begins (see page 130).

## 7 Teachers' notes

There are many opportunities for persuasive writing linked to other studies across the curriculum, e.g.:
- in science – when studying nutrition and health, leaflets or posters about healthy lifestyle
- in history – a visit to a historical site could lead to the production of an information leaflet to persuade others to visit

- in geography – environmental issues provide many contexts for expressing points of view and persuading others
- in music or art – persuading others why they should listen to a particular piece of music or look at a particular painting

Discussion, prior to writing, is an effective way of helping pupils to understand how to persuade. Time for brainstorming ideas will help to address the most common weakness of this form of writing, namely insufficient justification for the writer's point of view (see Activity 2). Encouraging the production of effective note-making using the formats recommended on page 121 will also help to ensure that the finished piece of writing addresses the issue of justification.

Effective note-making can also make the use of paragraphs clearer to pupils. The use of key points or bullet points gives a clear indication where new paragraphs are required. Persuasive writing benefits from effective paragraphs and, in conjunction with the use of the sheets provided, teachers should reinforce pupils' understanding of paragraphing when working on this form of writing. We also suggest that pupils are reminded to use connectives, such as *because* and *therefore*, in order to ensure that the writer's viewpoint is justified.

Teachers should note that Activity 2 is particularly helpful in meeting the NLS objectives for Years 4 and 5 which relate to planning and presenting a point of view.

We think teachers are unlikely to want to introduce Activity 3 before Year 6.

*Using the Success Sheets*

The Success Sheets provided at the end of this chapter (pages 143–4) are for writing essays. We have also included examples of Success Sheets 1 and 2 which have been adapted for writing book reviews (pages 145–6).

Once again the Success Sheets provided in this chapter contain a 'menu of possibilities' approach to the sentence starters provided in the 'Examples' column, allowing pupils to make their own choices. We believe that providing pupils with a range of examples is preferable as, by making choices, the pupils are encouraged to develop their own style of writing and are not inhibited by a single example. The model we have provided for writing persuasive essays is equally effective when applied to pupils presenting a point of view in a discussion or debate.

The Success Sheets can be easily differentiated – for example, the teacher may wish to adapt the sheets so that there are more or fewer supporting arguments than those provided. For some pupils it may be more appropriate to provide only one or two supporting arguments or justifications for their viewpoint, whereas for other pupils it may be appropriate to set the challenge of providing four or five supporting arguments.

A further activity which helps to make explicit to pupils themselves how the Success Sheets improve their writing is to set them a persuasive writing task, such as writing a piece to persuade a motorway developer not to build a motorway over the school playing field. The initial piece of writing is then produced *without* any support. In the next lesson pupils use the Success Sheets to attempt the same piece of writing, thus producing 'Before' and 'After' versions of the same persuasive text. These can then be used to discuss how the SUCCESS Approach has improved their writing, thereby making these new gains in learning evident to pupils themselves. See pages 124 and 125 for an example of this.

*Recommended sequence of lessons*

1 Deconstruction of an appropriate example of the type of persuasive text to be produced by pupils. Activity 1 provides an example of the deconstruction of a persuasive essay, which would be appropriate for Year 6 pupils.

2 Brainstorming ideas for a persuasive essay (or other form of persuasive text), recording ideas and suggestions on a spider diagram (see Activity 2).

3 Modelling how to organise notes from the outcome of the brainstorm in preparation for the writing task.

4 Shared writing of the required persuasive text, and/or

5 Pupils plan their own persuasive writing using Success Sheet 1 and write their first draft.

6 Pupils evaluate their writing using Success Sheet 2.

7 Teacher provides feedback to pupils on their persuasive texts and evaluations – this can be done orally or in writing.

8 Teacher summarises what has been learned about this text form with class.

The above sequence needs to be approached flexibly, depending on the type of persuasive text the teacher wishes to cover and the capabilities of the class. The sequence provided is based on

Against the new motorway Ben S

I am writing to you to tell you about building the motorway.

1) There could be a crash that could injure a child or any living thing.

2) We would have less space to play or games which we normly play.

3) Are parents could disapove about the motorway and more are school.

4) If we kicked a ball on the road we won't be able to get it.

5) We won't be able to concentrate in class with all the noise.

6) They will have to cross the road to get into school.

7) If there is an increase of crashes that will be more dangerous for them.

8) If you kick a ball on the road it could cause a serious accident.

9) It would be dangerous for Nature and animals.

10) The playground would be full of children when there will only be a lot of room.

11) We wouldn't be able to run around because the motorway will take up most of our room.

12) It will scare the birds and will destroy are playing fields.

13) They will need to do building works which will be dangerous.

14) You could build it on hard which is for sale.

15) It will stop us doing P.E. outside.

*Work of pupil at Holy Trinity School, Blackburn with Darwen: before using the Success Sheets*

Why the motorway shouldn't be build near our school.

I wish to persuade you that it is a bad idea to build a motorway on our school property.

Without a doubt the strongest reason for thinking the is their could be serious injures involving a colision between a car and a child. Or it could seriously injure them but if it is a lorry they could die. How would you feel if you sent your child to school then next thing you now your child is in hospital.

Another reason for thinking this is if your paying for your child to go to school he won't be able to concentrate because of the noise from the cars. In addion if your windows are open the people in there cars would shout very unpleasent words or beep there horns.

Furthermore if your child kicks a ball on the road he won't be able to get back because the cars. Moreover if the ball gos under a wheel it will cause a very serious axident.

As above of that there will be a decrise traffic. Furthermore there will be less axidents in the town.

To sum up, I think that the motorway is still a bad thing. In conclusion I still think that the motorway is a bad thing because it will increase an injurey to a child or teacher.

*Work of pupil at Holy Trinity School, Blackburn with Darwen: after using the Success Sheets*

preparing pupils to write persuasive essays. The principles of the approach, however, may be applied by teachers whatever kind of persuasive outcome they are working on with pupils. There is a sequence of work by pupils at Litlemoor School, Oldham, on pages 139–42)

## 8 Activity suggestions

*Activity 1: Deconstructing an example of persuasive writing*

Pupils are given a copy of 'Save Everest from its climbers' (page 131) as a stimulus for discussion. The piece of writing conforms to the structural model used in the Success Sheets included in this chapter and provides a useful starting point for the investigation of persuasive writing and the subsequent development of the pupils' own skills in writing persuasively.

Interactive questioning will promote discussion of the ways in which the writer persuades the reader to his/her point of view regarding this issue:
- statement of the writer's viewpoint
- series of supporting arguments for this viewpoint
- recognition of alternative viewpoint(s)
- counter arguments against the alternative viewpoints
- reiteration of original viewpoint (in different words)
- use of paragraphing to separate each element of the essay
- correct use of commas within sentences to separate phrases or clauses
- use of broad range of causal connectives e.g. *in addition, moreover*
- use of appropriate technical vocabulary to support viewpoint e.g. *expeditions, aluminium ladders*
- use of words and phrases to link to alternative viewpoints, e.g. *however*
- reference to generalised human agents, e.g. *climbers, authorities*

*Activity 2: Brainstorming ideas for persuasive essay*

This activity works well in groups of four, with one member of the group acting as the scribe and recording all the ideas contributed. We would suggest using a spider diagram for this activity. At the centre of the spider diagram would be the single unequivocal statement of the subject e.g. 'Fox hunting should be banned'. The suggested organisation for this lesson is as follows:
- Each group is given a sheet with the statement at the centre (A3 sheets if possible).

- The spider diagram format and brainstorming 'rules' are explained to the pupils (i.e. how to arrange the information around the 'body' on 'legs', and record all suggestions without comment).
- Each group brainstorms all the reasons why they think fox hunting should be banned. When all ideas have been recorded round the statement 'body', the group then discuss the different suggestions, deciding which arguments carry most weight. At this point they may even choose to discard some arguments.
- Once they have decided which arguments to use and their relative importance, groups can then prioritise the supporting arguments. They have now established the order for the points in their presentation/paragraphs in their persuasive essay.

This form of writing first appears in Year 4 Term 3 of the NLF and initially it may be sufficient for pupils to consider persuasive writing from a single viewpoint, but pupils in Years 5 and 6 should begin to consider arguments for the other side and include these in their presentation. There are a number of ways of doing this:
- Groups could go on to discuss the counter arguments and prioritise these
- Half the class could be given A3 sheets with the counter proposition – 'Fox hunting should not be banned' and brainstorm the arguments for this proposition
- Arguments could be shared through the display of the brainstorm sheets
- Alternatively, groups with opposing viewpoints could merge and discuss the organisation of the form of persuasive writing to be produced

*Activity 3: Impersonal persuasive writing*

This activity can be undertaken with Year 6 pupils who have coped well with the personal sheets, using 'Save Everest from its climbers (1)', included in this chapter. The persuasive writing used in Activity 1 has been rewritten in an impersonal style, 'Save Everest from its climbers (2)' (page 133). A teacher-led comparison of the both examples provides a good starting point for pupils who are ready to write in an impersonal style.

We suggest that teachers allow pupils to rewrite an existing piece of their own persuasive writing in an impersonal style as a preliminary to writing a new persuasive piece in an impersonal style. The preliminary work outlined in Activity 2, brainstorming ideas, would provide an equally good starting point for pupils who are going to write in an impersonal style.

*Activity 4: Persuasive language*

Not all persuasive writing conforms to the model outlined in the Success Sheets. Book, film and television reviews, and advertisements are different. However, what all forms of persuasive writing have in common is the way writers use language to persuade, and their awareness of purpose and audience.

Once again, examining existing examples is a good prelude to asking pupils to write their own. We have provided examples of advertising text, book, film and TV reviews and a letter to a newspaper (pages 134–138), all of which can be used as starting points for discussion of a particular form. We suggest that the focus for discussions should be:
• the purpose of the piece of writing
• who the writing is aimed at
• the appropriateness of the language used to achieve the writer's purpose.

Some specific questions are included for each text type, but these are merely suggestions. Teachers will no doubt wish to supply their own examples of each text group and provide their own directly pertinent questions. Questions should encourage pupils to deconstruct the text as well as to adapt it themselves.

*Examples of advertising text*

*Suggested questions:*
• Which adjectives do the writers use to make each piece more persuasive? (e.g. 'stunning')
• How do the writers create strong visual images?
• Who would each advertisement appeal to and why? What kind of people does the writer think drink whisky? (Notice the hyphenated words in the whisky advertisement).
• How could you change the piece to appeal to a different audience? (e.g. changing 'The Ancient Isle of Greece' to make it appeal to the youth market)

Other appropriate activities:

NLF objective Year 4 Term 3 T25 (see page 119) can be met by activities designed to evaluate existing advertisements with pupils, before they write their own.
• The teacher photocopies or enlarges an advertisement.
• They discuss the advertisement, pointing out how it gains the reader's attention, the language used, the use of pictures, opinion versus fact and so on, and annotate the advertisement as points are discussed.

- Pupils work in pairs annotating a different advertisement.
- If each pair is given a different advertisement they can create a classroom display; or pupils can collect examples for themselves, annotate them and add them to a classroom display.
- After pupils have produced their own advertisement, they can evaluate them by annotating them in the same way.

*Examples of book, film and TV reviews*

Book reviews (page 135)

*Suggested questions:*
- How does the writer of these reviews immediately capture the reader's attention? (Use of a list sentence at the start of the *Muddle Earth* review.)
- Can you think of other ways that you might grab the reader's attention?

Film review (page 136)

Suggested questions:
- Why does the writer use a comparison at the end of the review?
- Can you think of an alternative way of ending this piece that would be equally powerful?

Television review (page 137)

*Suggested questions:*
- Pick out the words that show the reviewer thinks this programme is worth watching.
- She thinks some children may enjoy this programme more than others. Which sentence tells us this?
- How does the writer personalise the review?
- What kind of programme is 'Feather Boy'? Which words and phrases tell us this?

Persuasive letter (page 138)

*Suggested questions:*
- The questions on Success Sheet 2: Persuasive Writing (page 144) are appropriate for this letter.

# Information Recording Grid (Persuasive writing)

Title: . . . . . . . . . . . . . . . . . . . . . . . . . . . . . . . . . . . . . . . . . . . . . . . .

| Key points (reasons for point of view) | Justification (details/examples/evidence) |
|---|---|
| | |
| | |
| | |
| | |
| | |
| | |

# Save Everest from its climbers (1)

I believe mountaineers should steer clear of Everest and seek out new challenges. I share Sir Edmund Hillary's point of view that there are now too many climbers attempting the world's highest peak. He was the first man to climb the mountain, but now I think it is appalling to see what is happening to Mount Everest.

Without a doubt there are too many expeditions setting out to climb the mountain. In my opinion the climbing of Everest has been devalued by the excessive number of expeditions setting out each year.

Another reason why I would wish to reduce the numbers climbing the mountain is the amount of rubbish which now clutters the mountain slopes. The mountain is littered with abandoned tents and climbing equipment. In 2001 a cleanup operation removed nearly 100 tonnes of rubbish from the mountain's slopes.

I have heard that more than 200 adventurers plan to climb Mount Everest this year. The authorities in Nepal have been forced to open up a second route up the mountain in order to avoid long queues of impatient climbers. I believe this can only increase the damaging impact on the environment.

Some people may think that if you can pay the £32,000 it costs to join an expedition, you should be free to climb as you wish. I think concern for the environment outweighs the selfish desire to boast you've climbed on Everest.

Moreover the mountain is not the challenge it once was. There are aluminium ladders bridging ice falls. There are thousands of metres of fixed ropes. In my view climbing Everest is becoming like joining a conducted tour.

At the same time there are many uncharted mountains waiting to be climbed. It may not be as glamorous as saying you've climbed Everest, but I'm sure you will agree there are still plenty of real challenges for people who want to climb mountains.

In conclusion, I think the number of expeditions setting out to climb on Everest should be restricted in order to protect the environment of this the world's highest peak.

adapted from an article by Iain S Bruce in the *Sunday Herald*, 13 April 2003

| Title | **Save Everest from its climbers (1)** | *Note use of persuasive language* |
|---|---|---|
| **Statement of the writer's viewpoint** | I believe mountaineers should steer clear of Everest and seek out new challenges. I share Sir Edmund Hillary's point of view that there are now too many climbers attempting the world's highest peak. He was the first man to climb the mountain, but now I think it is appalling to see what is happening to Mount Everest. | 'steer clear'<br><br><br><br><br>'appalling' |
| **Supporting argument 1** | Without a doubt there are too many expeditions setting out to climb the mountain. In my opinion the climbing of Everest has been devalued by the excessive number of expeditions setting out each year. | 'too many'<br><br><br>'excessive' |
| **Supporting argument 2** | Another reason why I would wish to reduce the numbers climbing the mountain is the amount of rubbish which now clutters the mountain slopes. The mountain is littered with abandoned tents and climbing equipment. In 2001 a cleanup operation removed nearly 100 tonnes of rubbish from the mountain's slopes. | 'clutters'<br>'littered with abandoned tents …' |
| **Supporting argument 3** | I have heard that more than 200 adventurers plan to climb Mount Everest this year. The authorities in Nepal have been forced to open up a second route up the mountain in order to avoid long queues of impatient climbers. I believe this can only increase the damaging impact on the environment. | 'forced'<br><br><br>'damaging impact' |
| **Counter argument** | Some people may think that if you can pay the £32,000 it costs to join an expedition, you should be free to climb as you wish. I think concern for the environment outweighs the selfish desire to boast you've climbed on Everest. | 'should be free'<br>'concern'<br>for … selfish desire … boast.' |
| **Supporting argument 4** | Moreover the mountain is not the challenge it once was. There are aluminium ladders bridging ice falls. There are thousands of metres of fixed ropes. In my view climbing Everest is becoming like joining a conducted tour. | 'not the challenge'<br><br><br><br>'conducted tour' |
| **Supporting argument 5** | At the same time there are many uncharted mountains waiting to be climbed. It may not be as glamorous as saying you've climbed Everest, but I'm sure you will agree there are still plenty of real challenges for people who want to climb mountains. | 'glamorous'<br>'plenty of real challenges' |
| **Reiteration of original viewpoint** | In conclusion, I think the number of expeditions setting out to climb on Everest should be restricted in order to protect the environment of this the world's highest peak. | 'restricted'<br>'protect'<br>'should seek out' |

adapted from an article by Iain S Bruce
in the *Sunday Herald*, 13 April 2003

# Save Everest from its climbers (2)

Mountaineers should steer clear of Everest and seek out new challenges. There are now too many climbers attempting the world's highest peak. It is appalling to see what is happening to Mount Everest.

Without a doubt there are too many expeditions setting out to climb the mountain. The climbing of the mountain has been devalued by the excessive number of expeditions setting out each year.

Another reason for wishing to reduce the numbers climbing the mountain is the amount of rubbish which now clutters the mountain slopes. The mountain has become littered with abandoned tents and climbing equipment. In 2001 a cleanup operation removed nearly 100 tonnes of rubbish from the mountain's slopes.

More than 200 adventurers plan to climb Mount Everest this year. The authorities in Nepal have been forced to open up a second route up the mountain in order to avoid long queues of impatient climbers. This can only increase the damaging impact on the environment.

Some people may think that if people can pay the £32,000 it costs to join an expedition, they should be free to climb as they wish. However, concern for the environment should outweigh the people's selfish desire to boast they've climbed on Everest.

Moreover the mountain is not the challenge it once was. There are aluminium ladders bridging ice falls. There are thousands of metres of fixed ropes. Climbing Everest is becoming like joining a conducted tour.

At the same time there are many uncharted mountains waiting to be climbed. It may not make for such a glamorous claim as having climbed Everest, but there are still plenty of real challenges for people who want to climb mountains.

In conclusion, there is no doubt that the number of expeditions setting out to climb on Everest should be restricted in order to protect the environment of this the world's highest peak.

# ADVERTISING TEXT

## 1  The Ancient Isle of Greece

Crete, the largest of the Greek Islands, boasts its own distinctive culture and varied landscape. From the fertile plains to huge gorges and snow-capped mountains evidence of ancient Minoan civilisation is scattered throughout the island. The towns and villages of Crete retain much of their ancient character. Visit the medieval Venetian harbour towns of Heraklion and Chania and the stunning archaeological sites including Knossos and Phaestos.

*This is from an advertisement for a holiday which also includes holiday costs and information plus pictures of Crete.*

## 2  Old Pulteney

Caithness is a truly magical place, a mix of moor, farmland and stunning coastline. It rims the edge of the magnificent Flow Country – home to the hen harrier, golden plover and red-throated diver – a place where shimmering boundaries between water and land are hard to discern.

It is from here that the Pulteney Distillery, standing by the ruined cliff top castle of the Auld Man of Wick, sources its life-enhancing water. This clear water with its faint infusion of rich peat is behind the smooth malt that is Old Pulteney, a malt popular with even those who profess not to like whisky, thanks to the sweet-tasting water sourced from a number of nearby lochs.

There is probably no other area in the world like the Flow Country with its myriad of lochans, and there are few distilleries that can boast such a magnificent setting as overlooking the harbour at Wick.

*From an advertisement for a brand of whisky, which included pictures of the Flow country and of the whisky itself.*

# BOOK REVIEWS

## Muddle Earth
by Paul Stewart and Chris Riddell

*Muddle Earth* has a floating lake, cry-baby ogres, pink stinky hogs and one wizard with one spell to call a warrior hero.

Enter Joe Jefferson, a schoolboy from ordinary earth. Our hero, once kitted out in the Wellies of Power and the Helmut of Sarcasm (a saucepan), must battle for the rights of good over the evil Dr Cuddles of Giggle Glade. If you have read *The Edge Chronicles* you will not be disappointed; if you haven't, you will read them after this.

Keeley Wilby

## George's Marvellous Medicine
by Roald Dahl

*George's Marvellous Medicine* isn't hard to read – who am I kidding, a five year old could read this standing on his head. Seriously, this is a very easy book.

The story line is like a fairy tale and the characters are too. Grandma (the wicked witch of the west), George (helpless, little, vulnerable, average boy) George's parents (the unknowing daughter and son-in-law) and, last but not least, the bugs (innocent little creatures devoured one by one by Grandma).

Roald Dahl's style of writing is exaggerated in this book and I would recommend it for younger children no more than six. I have read other Roald Dahl books and they were great, but *George's Marvellous Medicine*, well, it's just not as good.

Year 4 pupil

# FILM REVIEW

*National Security*

The flimsily plotted, witless 'National Security' is a dim descendant of the Eddie Murphy comedy thrillers, '48 Hours' and 'Beverly Hills Cop'. The black stand-up comic, Martin Lawrence, stars unappealingly as a chirpy, motormouthed braggart from South Central who's thrown out of the LAPD academy and then has a dedicated white cop (the endearing Steve Zhan) jailed on a false charge of brutality.

The two reluctantly join forces when, as serving guards for the security company of the title, they hunt down a band of thieves who have stolen some precious alloy for a foreign power. Eric Roberts plays the chief villain, but even if sister Julia had been cast in this role, she couldn't save this movie. It's so bad that by comparison it makes Beverly Hills Cop III look as good as Beverly Hills Cop II.

Philip French, *Observer*, 23 March 2003

# TELEVISION REVIEW

# FEATHER BOY

Winner of the 2002 *Blue Peter* Book of the Year awards Nicky Singer's children's novel comes to the screen in a compelling adaptation by Peter Tabern, who won a Bafta for CBBC's *Stig of the Dump*. Thomas Sangster, recently seen in *Love Actually*, is well cast as the 'nerdiest of the nerds', Robert Nobel, nicknamed Norbert NoBottle. Intimidated by school bully Niker and hopelessly in love with classmate Kate, Robert lives much of his life in fear. At home, his father has left and his mother, sympathetically played by former *EastEnder* Lindsey Coulson, is bitter about his new set-up with another woman.

Robert would like just about every aspect of his life to change, but he is unprepared for the adventures that befall him after a class trip to an old people's home. Adopted by a charismatic old lady (Sheila Hancock), he is beaten down by her chilling insistence that he visit a certain house. Ronald Pickup co-stars as her mysterious husband who has a habit of catching Robert's eye.

With its atmospheric, psychic dream sequences, this powerful drama was dubbed 'scary and weird' by my eight-year-old daughter, but my slightly older children may well find themselves hooked from the outset.

*Observer*, March 2004

# Letter to the editor of Anytown Gazette

Dear Sir

I am writing in support of the plan to build a by-pass round the town. I strongly believe that this is in the best interest of all of us who live here.

The main reason why I think this will be good for the town is that the volume of traffic which passes through the town centre is causing damage to houses and shops. The number of heavy vehicles has doubled in the past five years and our roads were never built to take such traffic. The constant rumbling of vehicles is shaking buildings to their foundations. The problem of the tower on the Parish church is just one example of the damage being caused.

Furthermore the streets are too narrow. In the High Street in particular, traffic is often at a standstill as two large vehicles attempt to squeeze past each other. Sometimes lorries mount the pavement to get past. How would you feel if you were a mother wheeling a pram along a pavement when a lorry mounts the pavement just ahead of you?

Another serious reason for building a by-pass is the danger our children and old people have to face. The number of vehicles makes accidents more likely, especially for those who cannot move quickly when crossing the road.

Some people may argue that there will be a drop in trade in the town's shops if drivers use the by-pass. I think it is so unpleasant shopping on our busy streets, because of exhaust fumes and the problem of getting across the road, that this is not really the case. I am sure more people will want to visit the town centre shops if the volume of traffic is reduced.

To sum up: we need the by-pass to make our town a cleaner, quieter and safer place for all.

Yours faithfully


Anthony Brown

Learning Objective :- To write persuasively

Oldham council plan to build a motorway through littlemoor school grounds. Write a piece persuading them not go a head-

If you build a motorway our school will be ruined Because the will be no place to play football. There will be loads of rubbish on the flow like fags and bottles of pop. There will be to much steam coming of the cars. There will be more robberies in the school. The infants could get run over and badly hurt. And there will be loads of smoke and fume coming of the cars. There could be petrol causes and they could set on fire. Theres already could be to main Roads near us and we dont need another. There could be more accidents and the cars might slip of the road. So dont make a motorway please dont because theres already two busy roads near us.

*This piece of persuasive writing was produced before using the Success Sheets. The pupil has many ideas but the structure of the piece does not enhance the persuasive argument.*

**SHEET 1 : PERSUASIVE WRITING**
**IDEAS DRAFT (with examples)**

| Features | Think about! | Examples |
|---|---|---|
| My point of view (What I think) | Clearly state your point of view in the first (or first two) sentences. Write in the first person. (Use 'I'.) | I want to argue that.... I strongly believe that.... I wish to persuade you that ...... |
| Supporting arguments for my point of view 1 (Reasons why I think this) | Use your strongest argument first. Express this in one or two sentences. Expand your strongest argument by adding details or examples. Use questions to involve the readers' emotions. | Without a doubt the strongest/main reason for thinking this is .... Unquestionably the key supporting argument is .... How would you feel if ....? Would you like this to ......? |
| Supporting arguments for my point of view 2 | Start a new paragraph for your next strongest argument. Use a variety of linking words to connect your ideas. | Another reason for thinking this is ..... Similarly ..... In addition ..... |
| Supporting arguments for my point of view 3 | Start a new paragraph for my next strongest argument. Use different linking words to connect your ideas. | Moreover.... Furthermore ..... |
| Other points of view 1 | Start a new paragraph. Explain why other people might think differently. | Other people might argue that ..... However,other people believe...... Nevertheless some people still hold to the view ... |
| Other points of view 2 | (Optional) Give another reason why other people might think differently. | AS ABOVE |
| Why I still hold my point of view | Summarise your main reasons for your point of view - no details or examples this time. Use different words to repeat your strongest argument. Use appropriate words to show this is your final paragraph. | To sum up, I think X because: • 1 • 2 • 3 To summarise ...... In conclusion ...... |

*The same pupil now uses an early version of the Persuasive Writing Ideas Draft and even though there are errors (such as using all the sentence starters given in the 'Examples' column at the opening of the writing) the end result is already more effective.*

Thursday 3Rd october 2002

lo. To produce a well structured piece of persuasive
writing.        persuasive writing

I want to argue that it will be a dreadful
idea if you build a motorway in the school
grounds.

✓

without the doubt the main reason for this is
the danger. To their health and safety of the children
If any of the car fumes get in their lungs they
would have to be rushed to hospital. Also they
could suffer awful injurys like getting run over. How
would you feel if your had a motorway built threw
their school.  ✓

Another reason for thinking this is the noise pollution.
The children and teachers will get sick of the noise.
It will distract them if they're Trying to do
work. there will be lack of concentration for nearly
everyone
        ✓

Furthermore I think my other argument is No where
to play. The playground will not be as big Because
with the school Field gone there will be only a little
play area left. this isnt very fair to the children
who want to play.

                                              thraugh
More over other people might want a motorway threw the
school. Like the journeys will be a lot quicker for the school
Nevertheless Oldham could come a more popular place  ✓
if they build a motorway because of more visitors.
                to be continued on the next page

 A well thought out piece

*The draft is now used to develop a more complete piece of persuasive writing with paragraph breaks now evidenced – these relate to the use of lines to divide the ideas draft: a visual way of reinforcing paragraphing.*

## SHEET 4 : PERSUASIVE WRITING
## HOW WELL HAVE I DONE? - SELF ASSESSMENT / PREPARATION FOR REDRAFT

| Features | Have I thought about? | YES/ NO | Notes for redraft |
|---|---|---|---|
| My point of view (What I think) | Have I clearly stated my point of view in the first (or first two) sentences? | yes | I'm impressed with my opening |
| | Have I written in the first person? (Have I used 'I'?) | yes | |
| Supporting arguments for my point of view 1 (Reasons why I think this) | Have I used my strongest argument first? Is it expressed in one or two sentences? | yes | But Bc they could have be health problems. |
| | Have I expanded my strongest argument by adding details or examples? | yes | yes i did |
| | Have I used questions to involve the readers' emotions? | ' | But Next time i need some question marks |
| Supporting arguments for my point of view 2 | Have I started a new paragraph for my next strongest argument? Have I used different linking words to connect my ideas? | yes/no | I didnt use any questions. |
| Supporting arguments for my point of view 3 | Have I started a new paragraph for my next strongest argument? | yes | I used without the doubt |
| | Have I used different linking words to connect my ideas? | yes | I think my ideas are good. (I used without the doubt) |
| Other points of view 1 | Have I started a new paragraph? Have I explained why other people might think differently? | yes | (another reason other people could think differently.) |
| Other points of view 2 | Have I given another reason why other people might think differently? | yes/no | Another reason other people could think differently. |
| | (You don't have to include this if you don't wish to.) | no | |
| Why I still hold my point of view | Have I used to different words to repeat my strongest argument? | yes | I used a virity or words. |
| | Have I used words to show this is my final paragraph? | No | Next time i will use to sum-up ?? |

How I feel about my piece of work :

*The self-assessment demonstrates that even after only one use of the Success Sheets the pupil is able to identify key areas for improvement – '… next time I need some question marks!'*

# SUCCESS SHEET 1: PERSUASIVE WRITING: *Ideas draft*

| Features | Think about! | Example | My own examples |
|---|---|---|---|
| *My point of view* | Clearly state your point of view in the first, or first two, sentences. Write in the first person 'I'. | I strongly believe mountaineers should … I want to argue that … I wish to persuade you that … | |
| *First argument supporting my point of view* | Use your strongest argument first. Express this in one or two sentences. Expand your strongest argument by adding details or examples. Use questions to involve the reader's emotions. | Without a doubt there are too many expeditions setting out … The main reason for thinking this is … Unquestionably the key argument is … How would you feel if … Would you like this to … | |
| *Second argument* | Start a new paragraph for your next strongest argument. Expand your argument by giving examples or details. Use a variety of linking words or phrases to connect your ideas. | Another reason why I would wish to reduce the numbers climbing …. Similarly … In addition … | |
| *Third argument* | Start another new paragraph for the argument you think is third in importance. Don't forget examples/details. Vary your choice of linking words or phrases to connect your ideas. | Moreover the mountain is not the challenge it once was … Furthermore … | |
| *Counter argument* | Start another new paragraph. Explain why other people might think differently/hold a different point of view. | Some people think that … Other people might argue that … However, other people believe … Nevertheless there are those who … | |
| *Summary of my point of view* | Summarise the main reasons for holding your point of view – no details or examples this time. Repeat your strongest argument using different words this time. Use appropriate words to show this is your final paragraph. | In conclusion, I think the number of expeditions … To sum up, I think … To summarise … | |

# SUCCESS SHEET 2: PERSUASIVE WRITING: *How well have I done?*

| Features | Have I thought about? | YES/NO | Notes for redrafting |
|---|---|---|---|
| *My point of view* | Is my point of view clearly stated in the first, or first two, sentences? Have I written in the first person 'I'? | | |
| *First argument supporting my point of view* | Have I used my strongest argument first? Is it expressed in one or two sentences? Have I expanded my strongest argument by adding details or examples? Have I used questions to involve the reader's emotions? | | |
| *Second argument* | Have I started a new paragraph for my next strongest argument? Have I expanded my argument by giving examples or details? Have I used a variety of linking words or phrases to connect my ideas? | | |
| *Third argument* | Have I started another new paragraph? Have I remembered examples/details? Have I varied my choice of linking words or phrases? | | |
| *Counter argument* | Have I started a new paragraph? Have I explained why other people might hold a different point of view? | | |
| *Summary of my point of view* | Have I summarised the main reasons for my point of view – no details or examples this time? Have I repeated my strongest argument using different words this time? Have I used appropriate words to show this is my final paragraph? | | |

# SUCCESS SHEET 1: PERSUASIVE WRITING/BOOK REVIEW: *Ideas draft*

| Features | Think about! | Example | My own examples |
|---|---|---|---|
| *Your opinion* | Clearly state your opinion in the first, or first two, sentences. Write in the first person 'I'. | I think everyone should read ****. It's the best book I've read this year. Although this is not **'s best book, it is still worth reading. | |
| *First reason for your opinion* | Choose your favourite aspect (think about plot, characters, setting, dialogue). Say what you think in one or two sentences. Don't forget to add details or examples. | What makes this book so enjoyable is … The main reason why I say this is … The best part is where … This is because … | |
| *Second reason* | Start a new paragraph for the next aspect. Say what you think in one or two sentences. Don't forget to add details or examples. Use a variety of linking words to connect your ideas. | The characters are … My favourite character is … I like him/her because … Another reason is … | |
| *Third reason* | Start another new paragraph. Don't forget examples/details. Use different linking words or phrases. | I liked the illustrations because … The book is funny/scary Another interesting thing is … Also … | |
| *Other opinions* | Start another new paragraph. Explain why other people might think differently/hold a different point of view. | Other people might not agree … However, there are some people who … There are other people who think **'s books are …, but I think they will … | |
| *Summary of your opinion* | Summarise the main reasons for holding your point of view – no details or examples this time. Use language to persuade the reader of your point of view OR invite them to make up their own mind. | In conclusion, you must read ** because … To sum up, I think … Read **** for yourself and decide if you think … | |

# SUCCESS SHEET 2: PERSUASIVE WRITING/BOOK REVIEW: *How well have I done?*

| Features | Have I thought about? | YES/NO | Notes for redrafting |
|---|---|---|---|
| *Your opinion* | Have I clearly stated my opinion in the first, or first two, sentences? <br> Have I written in the first person 'I'? | | |
| *First reason for your opinion* | Plot, characters, setting, dialogue <br> Have I used my favourite aspect first? <br> Have I expressed this in one or two sentences? <br> Have I expanded my strongest reason by adding details or examples? | | |
| *Second reason* | Have I started a new paragraph for my next reason? <br> Have I expanded my reason by giving examples or details? <br> Have I used a variety of linking words or phrases to connect my ideas? | | |
| *Third reason* | Have I started another new paragraph? <br> Have I included examples/details? <br> Have I varied my choice of linking words to connect ideas? | | |
| *Other opinions* | Have I started another new paragraph? <br> Have I explained why other people might hold a different point of view? | | |
| *Summary of your opinion* | Have I summarised the main reasons for my point of view ? <br> Have I used language to persuade the reader to my point of view or invited them to make up their own mind? | | |

# 7 Writing discussions

## 1 Definition

Discussions present two or more opposing arguments with equal weight and allow the reader to use all the arguments to reach a balanced judgement on the subject under discussion.

## 2 NLS Framework links

### Year 6 Term 2

- **T19** 'to write a balanced report of a controversial issue:
    - summarising fairly the competing views;
    - analysing strengths and weaknesses of different positions'

## 3 Text level features (purpose and organisation)

*Organisation*
We suggest the following two ways of organising discussion writing:

*Type 1*: the first form groups all supporting arguments for the initial viewpoint first, then does the same for the opposing arguments for the alternative viewpoint;

*Type 2*: the second form alternates the arguments supporting the different viewpoints throughout the discussion.

## 4 Sentence level features (style, punctuation and grammar)

*Style*
- statement of the issue for discussion at the beginning
- summary statement of the main points of view at the start
- use of impersonal tone
- use of summarising final paragraph

*Punctuation*
- use of paragraphs to separate viewpoints or balance arguments

*Grammar*
- consistent use of the present tense
- avoid use of the first person

## 5 Word level features (vocabulary, spelling)

*Vocabulary*
- use of range of additive connectives – e.g. *also, too, additionally*

- use of words and phrases to link to alternative viewpoints –
  e.g. *however, moreover, although, on the other hand*

*Spelling*
- technical language relating to the issue for discussion

## 6 Note-making and discussion writing

The most important note-making technique to be taught in
relation to writing discussions is the use of information
recording grids which allow key points for opposing points of
view to be noted (Information Recording Grid A, page 158). It is
a useful tool for organising arguments; the completed grid
provides an overview of the arguments and enables pupils to
check that they have sufficient information to do justice to both
viewpoints. The completed grid may also be used by pupils to
assess the relative weight or importance of the different
arguments which will enable them to structure their discussion
effectively e.g. deciding which is their strongest argument and
deciding to use it first. This can be done simply by numbering
items on the grid.

The completed grid also helps pupils to decide which text
organisation they think will be most effective for their discussion,
Type 1 or Type 2 (see page 159). They can then use the information
contained on their grid to write a well-structured discussion.

If pupils are aware that a viewpoint may be held by different
groups of people for different reasons, this information can also
be recorded on a grid (Information Recording Grid B, page 160)
and used to give more weight to the arguments presented (see
the references to e.g. 'the local MP' in the sample text used in
Activity 2). Another visual way of recording different points of
view held by different people is to use speech bubbles.

## 7 Teachers' notes

Teachers should note that although there are no specific NLF
references to discussion writing objectives before Year 6, there
are strong links with persuasive writing, and teaching of this
form culminates in the production of written discussion in Term
2 of Year 6:
- Year 4 Term 3 T21 and 23 – assembling and sequencing points
  to present a point of view;
- Year 5 Term 3 T19 – constructing an argument, presenting and
  evaluating it;
- Year 6 Term 2 T18 – constructing effective arguments, followed
  by Term 2 T19 – writing a balanced report of a controversial
  issue.

148

There are clearly similarities between writing texts which persuade and writing texts which discuss points of view. The main difference between them, however, is that effective discussion will present two or more opposing arguments with equal weight, allowing the reader to use all the arguments to reach a balanced judgement. The use of emotive language, often a key feature of persuasive writing, is not appropriate when writing discussions.

Pupils will encounter many controversial issues in school and beyond, and it is important that they learn how to make a balanced judgement of such issues. There are opportunities to consider issues which arouse strong feelings and controversy across many curricular areas, e.g.

- in PSHE – bullying, school uniform
- in RE – racial and religious tolerance
- in history – past attitudes, e.g. to slavery, child labour, voting rights, the role of women
- in geography – environmental issues such as pollution or the effects of developments on an area

Some children's fiction deals with controversial issues which can provide a stimulus for oral and written discussion.

The Success Sheets included in Chapter 6, 'Persuasive writing', are used to assist pupils to create discrete paragraphs for each argument supporting a specific point of view. Teachers will note that in the Success Sheets provided in Chapter 7 we present two alternative models for discussion writing. Type 1 groups all supporting arguments for the initial viewpoint collectively, then does likewise for the opposing arguments for the alternative viewpoint. Type 2 provides pupils with a model in which arguments supporting viewpoints one and two are alternated. The central feature of both forms is that they ensure a balanced perspective of the arguments being presented.

Teachers may wish to discuss these alternative approaches to paragraphing explicitly, as they relate to the idea of beginning a new paragraph with each change of focus. It is important, however to allow pupils to decide for themselves which of the two forms they may wish to use for the specific discussion writing task they are being asked to complete.

Sentence starters are provided to encourage pupils to vary their choices and begin to choose and create their own. A useful differentiation device is to raise the readability level of the sentence starters included in the examples column e.g. Activity 2 has the given example, 'The issue being discussed is whether a motorway should be built on our lower playing field?' This could be adapted by the pupil to read, 'There are those who see the advantages of the proposed motorway, while others view the development with dismay.' This also accentuates the impersonal tone which is a feature of discussion writing.

In the frames provided we have assumed that those who support the arguments do so from a consistent point of view. More able pupils may be able to see that the same point of view may be held by different groups of people for different reasons e.g. using the motorway example, those in favour of the motorway could include motorists wanting faster access to their destination; school governors wishing to sell land to boost school funds; local councillors hoping to provide jobs and reduce unemployment figures; while those against might include pupils interested in sport; teachers concerned about increased noise levels interrupting lessons; environmentalists concerned about pollution from vehicle fumes.

*Recommended sequence of activities*

1 Discussion of IFD (Issue for Discussion) sentences and a short activity for pupils to shorten some overlong IFD sentences. (See Activity 1)

2 Deconstruction of an appropriate discussion text (an example, suitable for Year 6 pupils, is contained in Activity 2).

3 Modelling how to make notes using one of the Information Grid formats outlining opposing points of view (see Activity 3).

4 Shared writing of a discussion text, using the notes from the previous activity and the structural model covered during the deconstruction activity outlined on Success Sheet 1.

5 Pupils plan their own discussion writing using Success Sheet 1, and write their first draft. Pupils may write the first draft directly from notes on their Information Recording Grid, but they require Success Sheet 1 to provide the structure for the discussion.

6 Pupils evaluate their writing using Success Sheet 2.

7 Teacher provides feedback to pupils on their discussion texts and evaluations – this can be done orally or in writing.

8 Teacher summarises what has been learned about this text form with class.

In the sequence outlined in (3) and (4) above, teachers should not feel bound by the topic provided. They are free to provide their own topic for these activities.

## 8  Activity suggestions

*Activity 1: Editing overlong IFD sentences*

In this chapter we use the acronym IFD (Issue For Discussion) for this key aspect of the text form. A useful introductory activity is to encourage pupils to express issues concisely by reducing the number of words in examples of over-long IFD sentences (see page 155).

*Overlong IFD sentences. Possible answers and key teaching points*

1  Should ball games be banned in the playground? *(use of collective noun)*
2  Should a motorway be built near our school? *(reduction of detail)*
3  Should trees in the rain forest be cut down? *(elimination of examples)*
4  Is school uniform a good idea? *(changing the sentence starter)*
5  Should confectionery be banned from lessons? *(elimination of superfluous detail)*
6  When at school should pupils be quiet at all times? *(inappropriate use of simile)*
7  When should children watch television?  *(altering the sentence starter)*
8  What should children read? *(altering the sentence starter, omitting details)*

*Activity 2: Deconstructing an example of discussion writing*

Pupils are given a copy of 'Should motorway plans go ahead? Type 1' (see page 156) as a stimulus for discussion. The piece of writing conforms to the structural model used in the Success Sheets included in this chapter and provides a useful starting point for the investigation of discussion writing and the subsequent development of the pupils' writing skills.

Interactive questioning will promote discussion of the ways in which the writer presents each point of view:
• clear statement of the IFD (issue for discussion)
• both viewpoints are stated in the second paragraph, without arguments
• the structural organisation: presenting the arguments for viewpoint 1 and then for viewpoint 2

- use of paragraphs to separate each argument for and against
- presenting the strongest argument first
- use of different sentence starters
- using different linking words
- variety in the choice of connectives
- indicating range of sources supporting viewpoints
- emotive language
- open-ended concluding paragraph inviting the reader to make up his/her own mind

Pupils are then given a copy of 'Should motorway plans go ahead? Type 2' (see page 157) in order to study an alternative structure, namely, alternating arguments for both viewpoints within the same paragraph. Thus they have the opportunity to see the same information presented in two different ways. They can also see a different ending in which the writer states his/her own belief. Teachers could discuss with their pupils which structure they prefer, giving reasons for the choice they make, and similarly which ending they prefer and why.

The discussion example selected for this activity is long, but it illustrates most of the features of successful discussion writing and is included in its entirety for this reason. We do not expect pupils to write passages of this length.

*Activity 3: Using an information grid*

The importance of using an Information Recording Grid as preparation for discussion writing is outlined on page 148. We offer two formats for gathering information for opposing viewpoints, one of which allows pupils to indicate who holds the views being noted. We include examples of the notes made for the discussion piece used in Activity 2 using both grid formats (pages 158, 160). These could be used for discussion on the following issues:
- how to use the Information Recording Grids
- a reminder of the need to record only keywords and phrases when making notes
- how the notes have been expanded in the finished writing.

We would suggest teachers then model the use of one of the Information Grids for making notes on a topic they have selected for discussion writing as preparation for pupils writing a first draft (see Chapter 4, Activity 5).

Alternatively teachers might take one of the IFD sentences from Activity 1, page 155 and use it to model making notes on an Information Grid.

*Activity 4: Making notes*

The following is suggested as an alternative approach to making notes on an issue involving people who hold different points of view:

- Begin with the issue for discussion, e.g. 'Should motorway plans go ahead?' and brainstorm which groups of people might have a point of view on this issue.
- Record the results of the brainstorm on a spider diagram.
- Decide whether these various groups would be for or against the issue and add that information to the spider diagram. Results might be:

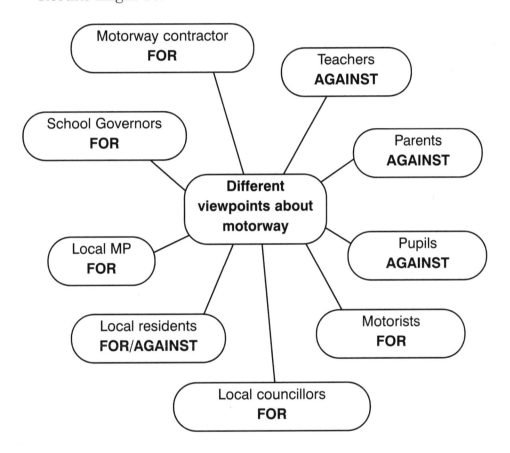

- Pupils then make notes on the reasons why people in these various groups would hold that point of view. Use either an amended version of the Information Recording Grid or the sheet containing blank speech bubbles (Information Recording Grid C or Notes/Speech Bubbles, pages 162–5).
- Once this has been done pupils will decide which structural model they wish to use. They will then be ready to decide on the ordering of their arguments, e.g. which reason is the most important, next in importance *or* which group's opinion carries most weight. Pupils should be aware that they make choices in organising their writing.

*Activity 5: Developing impartial, balanced writing*

We suggest that one way of approaching this task would be to take a strong piece of persuasive writing (this could be something written by an author, taken from a book or journal, written by the teacher or, best of all, the pupil's own earlier work) and construct counter arguments. Pupils would make notes of the arguments and counter-arguments on one of the Information Recording Grids, prior to writing a discussion of the issue.

We have provided a piece of persuasive writing that could be used for this activity (School uniform, page 166). Teachers should note that an important part of this task would be to change the personal (first person) style of this piece into an impersonal style.

# Overlong IFD sentences

*These sentences are too long. Can you make them shorter and better?*

1   Should games like football and basketball and cricket be stopped altogether in our playground or should we be allowed to play them and tennis as well?

   ........................................................................

   ........................................................................

2   Should building the motorway on our school fields and playground near our classrooms take place?

   ........................................................................

   ........................................................................

3   Should people cut down the trees in the rain forest to make logs and other timber things like furniture and toys or should they be left as they are?

   ........................................................................

   ........................................................................

4   Should pupils be made to wear school uniform all of the time so that they all look the same instead of being allowed to choose?

   ........................................................................

   ........................................................................

5   Should chewing gum, sweets, Mars bars, Milky Way, Snickers and other chocolate bars be banned from lessons so we don't eat in class?

   ........................................................................

   ........................................................................

6   Should we be forced to be as quiet as mice when lining up to come into school, in the corridors, during dinners as well as when we are working in the classroom?

   ........................................................................

   ........................................................................

7   Should television only be watched by schoolchildren between seven and nine o'clock at night or should it be watched at any time at all?

   ........................................................................

   ........................................................................

8   Should we be able to read comics or other things like magazines that we really like or should we only read books all of the time instead?

   ........................................................................

   ........................................................................

| Title | **TYPE 1: Should motorway plans go ahead?** | *Note:* Title short and precise |
|---|---|---|
| Clear statement of the issue for discussion | The issue being discussed is whether a motorway should be built on the school's lower playing field. | *Impersonal style, not 'I'* |
| Statement of different points of view | Some people think the building of the motorway will benefit the whole community, while others see it as a disaster for everyone in the long run. | *Both viewpoints stated* |
| First supporting argument for viewpoint 1 | Those who support the building of the motorway do so because it it will enable motorists to get to and from the centre of town more quickly. This will save them time on the journey. | *Strongest argument first* |
| Second supporting argument for viewpoint 1 | A further point they make is that the sale of the land for the motorway would provide a much-needed boost to school funds. The money would go a long way to providing up-to-date computing and sports equipment. | *Different sentence starter from previous paragraph* |
| Further supporting argument for viewpoint 1 | Furthermore they point out that the construction of the motorway will provide jobs in the area. This view is supported by the local MP, as well as many local councillors. They think the loss of playing fields is a small price to pay for reducing unemployment. | *Variety of connectives* |
| First supporting argument for viewpoint 2 | However, there are many people who oppose the motorway plan. They think that a motorway will bring increased traffic into the area which will lead to increased pollution which carries the danger of serious health risk for pupils and teachers. Exhaust fumes can cause asthma and other breathing problems. Teachers also worry that noise levels will interrupt lessons and make it difficult for pupils to concentrate on their work. | *Strongest argument for viewpoint 2*<br><br>*Different linking words for justification*<br><br>*Note range of sources supporting different viewpoints e.g. school governors, motorists, teachers* |
| Second supporting argument for viewpoint 2 | Furthermore they ask what is the point of improving sports equipment at the expense of the playing fields? The playing fields are well-used by all the school teams, particularly the football team, who have been top of the league for the last two seasons. Where will the teams practise in future if the motorway plan goes ahead? | *Different sentence starters from previous paragraph* |
| Further supporting argument for viewpoint 2 | Jobs building the motorway will only be short term, they also argue. Once construction of the motorway is over, the jobs will cease, but the motorway, with all the noise and pollution, will be here to stay, while the playing fields are lost to the school forever. | *Emotive language – 'school will be lost forever'* |
| Concluding paragraph inviting reader to make up his own mind | As you can see there are strong arguments to support both viewpoints. You will have to weigh them up and decide which viewpoint you support. | *Open-ended for reader to choose* |

| | | Note: |
|---|---|---|
| **Title**<br><br>**Clear statement of the issue for discussion** | **TYPE 2: Should motorway plans go ahead?**<br><br>The issue being discussed is whether or not a motorway should be built on the school's lower playing field. | *Title short and precise*<br><br>*Impersonal style, not 'I'* |
| **Statement of different points of view** | There are those who see the advantages of the proposed motorway, whilst others view the proposed development with dismay. | *Both viewpoints stated with no justification* |
| **First supporting argument for viewpoint 1**<br><br>**First supporting argument for viewpoint 2** | Many motorists support the building of the motorway because it will enable them to get to and from the centre of town more quickly. This will save them time on the journey. However, many people point out that a motorway will bring increased traffic into the area with all the pollution from exhaust fumes. Such pollution carries the danger of serious health risk for pupils and teachers. Exhaust fumes can cause asthma and other breathing problems. Teachers also worry that noise levels will interrupt lessons and make it difficult for pupils to concentrate on their work. | *Strongest arguments for each veiwpoint first, using different linking words which encourage justification for each – 'because', 'however'* |
| **Second supporting argument for viewpoint 1**<br><br>**Second supporting argument for viewpoint 2** | The school governors also support the plan because they see the sale of the land for the motorway as providing a much-needed boost to school funds. The money would go a long way to providing up-to-date computing and sports equipment. Those who oppose the plan ask what the point is of improving sports equipment at the expense of the playing fields. The playing fields are well-used by all the school teams, particularly the football team, who have been top of the league for the last two seasons. Where will they practise in future if the motorway plan goes ahead? | *Different sentence starters*<br><br><br><br><br><br>*Use of question to involve the reader* |
| **Further supporting argument for viewpoint 1**<br><br>**Further supporting argument for viewpoint 2** | Some people say that the construction of the motorway will provide jobs in the area. This view is supported by our local MP, as well as many local councillors. They think the loss of playing fields is a small price to pay for reducing unemployment. Against this is the fact that these jobs will be short term, but the motorway will be here to stay and the playing fields lost forever. | *Note range of sources supporting different viewpoints e.g. school governors, motorists, teachers, local M.P.* |
| **Concluding paragraph stating the author's own belief** | As you can see there are strong arguments to support both viewpoints. However, after weighing up all the arguments, I think the the motorway plan should be opposed, because in the long run the loss of the playing fields will be a disaster for the school. | *Ending which states writer's personal opinion* |

## INFORMATION RECORDING GRID A

**IFD:** ..........................................................................

| Viewpoint 1 | Viewpoint 2 |
|---|---|
| | |

# INFORMATION RECORDING GRID A

**IFD:** *Should motorway plans go ahead?* ...........................................................................

| Viewpoint 1 | Viewpoint 2 |
|---|---|
| • faster transport | • more traffic |
| • save time | • pollution |
| • more time with family | • health risks |
| | • noise |
| | • accidents/danger |
| • land sale = £ for school funds | • lose playing fields |
| • IT & PE equipment | • ? school football team's practice |
| • jobs for unemployed | • jobs short term |

## INFORMATION RECORDING GRID B

**IFD:** ...........................................................

| Viewpoint 1 | Who thinks this? | Viewpoint 2 | Who thinks this? |
|---|---|---|---|
| | | | |

## INFORMATION RECORDING GRID B

**IFD:** Should motorway plans go ahead? . . . . . . . . . . . . . . . . . . . . . . . . . . . . . . . . . . . . . . . . . . . . . . . . . . . . . . . . . .

| Viewpoint 1 | Who thinks this? | Viewpoint 2 | Who thinks this? |
|---|---|---|---|
| • faster transport<br>• save time<br>• more time with family | motorists | • more traffic<br>• pollution<br>• health risks<br>• noise<br>• accidents | pupils<br>most teachers<br>environmentalists<br><br>parents |
| • land sale £ for school funds<br>• IT & PE equipment | school governors and some teachers | • lose playing fields<br>• ? school football team's practice | pupils<br>most teachers |
| • jobs for unemployed | local MP and local councillors | • jobs short term | pupils<br>most teacher |

# INFORMATION RECORDING GRID C

**IFD:** Should motorway plans go ahead? ..............................................................

| FOR | REASONS | AGAINST | REASONS |
|---|---|---|---|
| • Motorway Contractor | Make money Provide jobs etc | • Pupils | |
| • Local MP | | • Parents | |
| • Motorists | | • Teachers | |
| • School Governors | | • Local Residents | |
| • Local Councillors | | | |
| • Local Residents | | | |
| | | | |

# INFORMATION RECORDING GRID C

**IFD:** . . . . . . . . . . . . . . . . . . . . . . . . . . . . . . . . . . . . . . . . . . . . . . . . . . . . . . . . . . . . . . . . . . . . . . . . . . . .

| FOR | REASONS | AGAINST | REASONS |
|---|---|---|---|
|  |  |  |  |
|  |  |  |  |
|  |  |  |  |
|  |  |  |  |
|  |  |  |  |
|  |  |  |  |
|  |  |  |  |

**NOTES**

**IFD:** ...Should motorway plans go ahead?...........

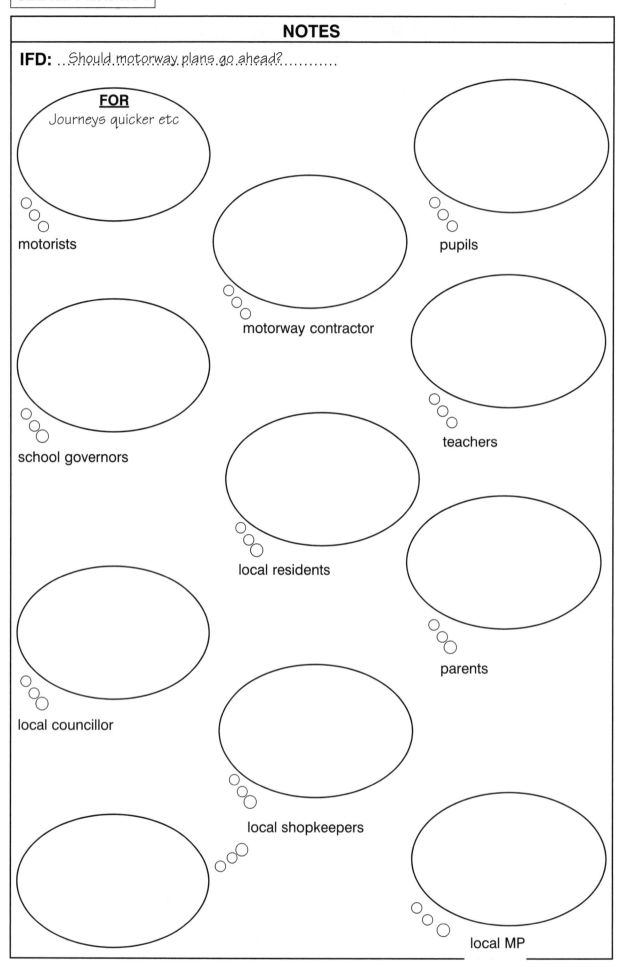

**FOR**
Journeys quicker etc

motorists

pupils

motorway contractor

school governors

teachers

local residents

parents

local councillor

local shopkeepers

local MP

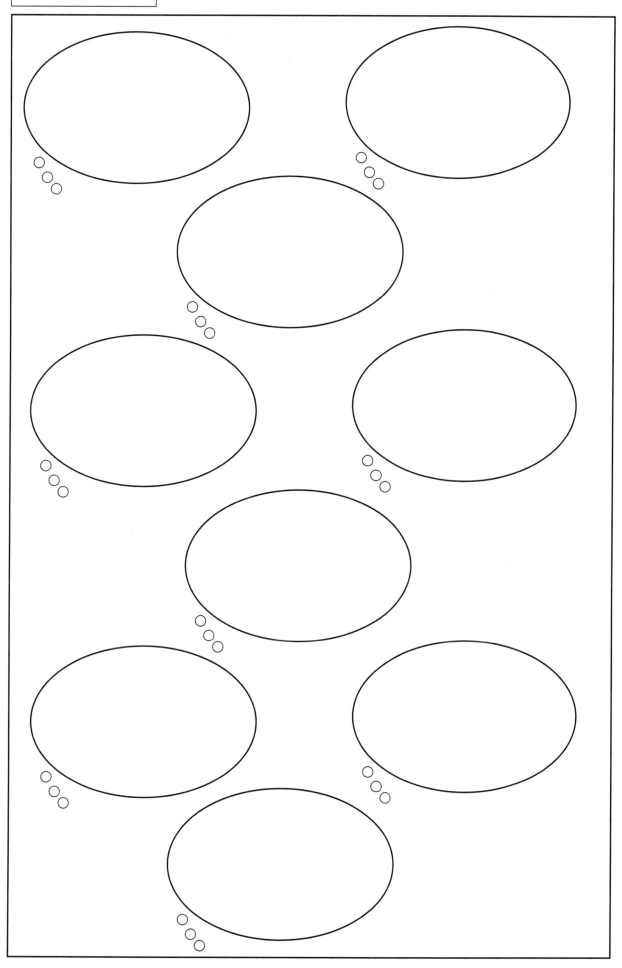

# School uniform

I strongly believe everyone should wear school uniform.

The main reason why I think this is that it makes everyone equal. In school uniform everyone looks the same so you cannot tell who can afford to buy designer clothes and who can't. It also stops people from trying to outdo each other in what they wear. How would you feel if you turned up at school and found everyone in better clothes than you?

I think everyone should be the same at school. After all, we're there to learn, not to take part in a fashion parade. It is much neater and tidier if everyone looks the same. I also think it makes you feel more a part of the school when everyone wears the same thing.

In addition it saves you time in the morning because you don't have to make choices. You know exactly what clothes to put on. If you could wear what you like, you might spend ages trying to choose what to wear each day.

Another good reason for wearing school uniform is that it gives you something to change out of when you get home from school. You can put on your comfortable jeans and trainers and really feel that school is over for the day. I like the feeling of difference between school and home.

In conclusion, I think school uniform is a very good thing and everyone should wear it.

# SUCCESS SHEET 1: DISCUSSION WRITING: *Ideas draft* (Types 1 and 2)

| Features | Think about! | Example | My own examples |
|---|---|---|---|
| (1) Title | Short version of the IFD | Should motorway plans go ahead? | |
| (2) Issues for discussion (IFD) | Tell the reader what the issue is about in as few words as possible. Do not write in the first person. (Don't use 'I'/'we') | The issue being discussed is … … whether or not a motorway should be built on the school's lower playing field. | |
| (3) Sentences stating the two different points of view | Cover each of the different points of view. Don't add supporting detail for or against. | Some people say …(Viewpoint 1) whilst others say …(Viewpoint 2) | |
| (4) Supporting arguments for Viewpoint 1 * | Remember to use a new paragraph for each argument. Use your strongest argument first. Use words like 'because' and 'therefore' to explain why people think this. Avoid repeating earlier arguments. | Those who support (Viewpoint 1) think that … They also think … | |
| 5) Supporting arguments for Viewpoint 2 * | Remember to use a new paragraph for each argument. Use your strongest argument first. Use different sentence starters to those used for Viewpoint 1. Don't forget 'because' and 'therefore' to explain why people think this. Avoid repeating earlier arguments. | Those who support (Viewpoint 2) think that … They also think … | |
| *Alternative organisation of (4) and (5) | **You could organise your discussion by alternating the supporting arguments for Viewpoints 1 and 2.** | | |
| (6) Conclusion A OR Conclusion B | Tell the reader there are strong arguments on both sides but conclude by telling the reader your point of view. Tell the reader there are strong arguments on both sides then invite the reader to make up his/her own mind. | As you can see there are strong arguments to support both viewpoints. However, after carefully weighing up all the arguments, I think … because As you can see there are strong arguments to support both viewpoints. You will have to decide for yourself which viewpoint you support. | |

# SUCCESS SHEET 2: DISCUSSION WRITING: *How well have I done?* – SELF ASSESSMENT (Types 1 and 2)

| Features | Have I thought about? | YES/NO | Notes for redrafting |
|---|---|---|---|
| (1) Title | Short version of the IFD | | |
| (2) Issues for discussion (IFD) | Have I told the reader what the issue is about in as few words as possible? Have I remembered not to write in the first person? ('I'/'we') | | |
| (3) Sentences stating the two different points of view | Have I covered each of the different points of view? Have I remembered not to add supporting detail for or against? | | |
| (4) Supporting arguments for Viewpoint 1 * | Have I remembered to use a new paragraph for each argument? Have I used my strongest argument first? Have I used words like 'because' and 'therefore' to explain why people think this? | | |
| 5) Supporting arguments for Viewpoint 2 * | Have I remembered to use a new paragraph for each argument for Viewpoint 2? Have I used my strongest argument first? Have I used words like 'because' and 'therefore' to explain why people think this? Have I avoided repeating earlier arguments? | | |
| *Alternative organisation of (4) and (5) | **Have I chosen to organise my discussion by alternating the supporting arguments for Viewpoints 1 and 2?** | | |
| (6) Conclusion A  OR  Conclusion B | Have I told the reader there are strong arguments on both sides? Have I concluded by telling the reader my point of view? Have I told the reader there are strong arguments on both sides? Have I then invited the reader to make up his/her own mind? | | |

# Appendix 1: Research and note-making skills

Increasingly in the complex world we find ourselves in, where people are likely to change jobs frequently during their working life and where lifelong learning is accepted as essential, the ability to handle information effectively is seen as a key factor for success.

Handling information effectively means being able to:
- locate the information required
- evaluate the accuracy and relevance of information found
- select what is required and make notes
- organise notes taken
- present and communicate the results of the research in the most appropriate form.

These skills are required by the Year 1 child researching the weather pattern during a school week through to the PhD student researching his thesis, so teachers need to be clear and thorough in discussing and reviewing these skills with their pupils each time such a task is undertaken. They are higher order thinking skills, which is why it is essential that teachers model these skills for their pupils. Sharing with pupils the thought processes involved in carrying out research and making notes, enables them to understand and internalise these thought processes for themselves over time, so that, over time, they become routine.

## Locating information

To be able to do this effectively pupils need to be taught, through demonstration and modelling:
- to identify and record keywords
- how to use the library system
- how to find information efficiently using skimming, scanning and search reading
- how people are potential sources of information
- how to access information using IT sources.

## Evaluating the accuracy and relevance of information

To be able to do this effectively pupils need to:
- understand the subject of their research
- understand the purpose of their research
- check information against their keywords
- check the date of publications to see if they are out of date
- check sources of the information – could this one be biased?
- have the process of evaluating information demonstrated and modelled for them.

## Selecting what is required

Pupils often find it difficult to be selective in the information they extract, particularly from books, and often end up copying (or downloading) large extracts. To be able to select information effectively pupils need to:
- be shown how to match the information they extract to their requirements
- be given or draw up a list of questions requiring answers to frame their research
- identify keywords.

## Making notes

To be able to do this effectively pupils need to be taught, through demonstration and modelling, to:
- always write keywords and phrases, not complete sentences
- seek further clarification when necessary
- use abbreviations
- use space
- use techniques to make things stand out – colour, block capitals, lists and so on
- use diagrams and patterns to make information clear and provide a visual prompt
- keep a note of sources so that they can be found again
- use their own words where possible.

## Organising notes

This is particularly important when pupils are gathering information from a range of sources and when they are using their notes to write a first draft. It is be helpful to encourage pupils to:
- make notes on separate cards or post-its so they can be rearranged easily
- organise their notes under headings
- take time to go over notes and reorganise them if necessary.

## Presenting and communicating results

Within the context of this book, the results of pupils' research will be communicated in one or other of the non-fiction text forms, but teachers will provide opportunities for their pupils to present their findings in a wider range of ways:
- oral presentations such as class talks, contributions to debates, radio programmes, dramatisations etc.
- visual displays of work including text, pictures, captions, diagrams, notes etc.
- contributions to class books, leaflets etc.

What teachers are expected to cover in Key Stages 1 and 2 is clearly outlined in the NLF objectives. The progression expected in research and note-making skills can be found in objectives which have been set for reading comprehension and writing for each year group. Throughout the chapters in this book, we attempt to indicate suitable note-making techniques and formats for each of the text forms covered and to address the NLF objectives appropriately.

A photocopiable sheet designed to remind pupils of key aspects of research and note-making skills follows at the end of this appendix. This could be used as an aide-memoire with pupils from Year 3 onwards as it covers many of the objectives set for that year group.

This is followed by a practical note-making activity designed to remind pupils of the reasons why taking notes is important and how notes can help them. This activity could be used with Year 3 pupils or at any time when the teacher thinks pupils would benefit from a reminder of the importance of note-making. The text is an example of the Explanation genre and could also be used placing the emphasis of the activity on explanations.

# Effective note making

| Reading/note-making strategy | How to carry it out | When it is appropriate |
|---|---|---|
| **Selecting a book** | Use the blurb, contents, chapter headings to see what is in the book, check publishing date, check if there is an index and useful illustrations. Read a bit to see if you are going to understand the book. | When you want to **check the usefulness** of a book |
| **Skimming** | You do not read every word but look at chapter headings, first and last paragraphs, illustrations, diagrams. The aim is to find out if the information is relevant to your needs. | To gain a **general impression** of what the material is about; to get the gist of something |
| **Scanning** | As you search for specific information you allow your eyes to run very quickly over the page . You don't read every word, but scan quickly till your brain recognises what it is looking for. Clues in books – preface, contents, chapter headings, paragraph headings, index, names, titles etc.<br><br>NB YOU NEED A KEYWORD TO SCAN | To find a **specific piece of information** |
| **Search reading** | You read carefully and thoughtfully. You ask questions as you read; you go back to check points; you might use techniques such as highlighting, underlining and note-taking to help you to retain the information. | To gain **complete understanding**. |
| ~~Note-taking~~ | You need specific questions to frame your research and keep your notes relevant.<br><br>In making notes remember:<br>• always write keywords and phrases, *not* complete sentences<br>• use abbreviations where possible<br>• use space to make notes clear<br>• use techniques to make things stand out – colour, block capitals, lists and so on<br>• use diagrams or patterns to help you remember<br>• keep a note of your sources so that you can go back to them<br>• use your own words where possible<br>• take time to go over notes, organise them under headings so that you can find what you need easily. | To **retain information** for future use |

# Why is it important to make notes?

I want to explain why I think making notes is important.

The main reason is that it gives me a record of the things I need to remember. It is important that notes are brief and to the point, so that I don't have so much written down that I never have time to read them.

Another reason is that the actual making of the notes helps me to remember what I have written down. In addition I have the notes themselves to jog my memory and remind me of the lesson or research.

Also making notes helps me to understand what I'm learning. To make notes, I have to pick out the key points and jot them down. I can't do this if I haven't understood what the lesson is about.

I like to make notes in diagrams, usually flow charts or spider diagrams. I find putting my thoughts down on paper like this helps me to check that I really have understood the lesson. And if I haven't understood it properly, I can go and ask or look for further information. In this way, making notes helps me to learn more effectively.

I like to use notes when I'm writing a story or some other piece of writing. It helps to organise my thoughts and makes for a better piece of writing. I also use notes if I have to give a talk to the class or take part in a debate. I don't forget important points if I have notes to remind me.

Finally, I find my notes are really helpful when I have to do homework or revise for tests. I wouldn't have time to read everything before doing homework or a test, so my notes are really important.

So you can see why I think it is important to make notes.

**Pick out the keywords or phrases in the above passage and make a list in note form of the reasons why you should make notes.**

# Appendix 2: Progression in research and note-making skills in the NLS framework

| READING COMPREHENSION | WRITING |
|---|---|
| **YEAR 1**<br><br>**Term 2**<br>**T20** to use simple dictionaries and to understand their alphabetical organisation<br><br>**T21** to understand the purpose of contents pages and indexes and to begin to locate information by page numbers and words by initial letter | **Term 2**<br>**T22** to write labels for drawings and diagrams<br><br>**T23** to produce extended captions<br><br>**T25** to assemble information from own experience ... to organise in lists |
| **Term 3**<br>**T17** to recognise that non-fiction books on similar themes can give different information and present information in different ways<br><br>**T19** to identify simple questions and use text to find answers. To locate parts of texts that give particular information including labelled diagrams and charts | **Term 3**<br>**T22** to write own questions prior to reading for information and to record answers |

| READING COMPREHENSION | WRITING |
|---|---|
| **YEAR 2** | |
| | **Term 1**<br><br>**T17** to use diagrams in instructions |
| **Term 2**<br>**T18** to use other alphabetically ordered texts, eg indexes, directories, listings, registers; to discuss how they are used<br><br>**T19** to read flow charts and cyclical diagrams that explain a process | **Term 2**<br>**T21** to produce simple flow charts or diagrams that explain a process |
| **Term 3**<br>**T14** to pose questions and record these in writing, prior to reading non-fiction to find answers<br><br>**T15** to use a contents page and index to find way about text<br><br>**T16** to scan a text to find specific sections, eg key words or phrases, subheadings<br><br>**T17** to skim-read title, contents page, illustrations, chapter headings and sub-headings, to speculate what a book might be about<br><br>**T18** to evaluate the usefulness of a text for its purpose | **Term 3**<br>**T19** to make simple notes from non-fiction texts, eg key words and phrases, page references, headings |

| READING COMPREHENSION | WRITING |
|---|---|
| **YEAR 3**<br><br>**Term 1**<br>**T18** to locate information, using contents, index, headings, sub-headings, page nos., bibliographies<br><br>**T19** to compare the way information is presented, e.g. by comparing a variety of information texts including IT-based sources<br><br>**T20** to read information passages, and identify main points or gist of text, e.g. by noting or underlining key words or phrases, listing the 4 or 5 key points covered | **Term 1**<br>**T21** to make a simple record of information from texts read, e.g. by completing a chart of information discovered, by listing key words, drawing together notes from more than one source<br><br>**T22** … using notes made to organise and present ideas |
| | **Term 2**<br>**T17** to make clear notes through, e.g.<br>• discussing the purpose of note-making and looking at simple examples<br>• identifying the purpose for which particular notes will be used<br>• identifying key words, phrases and sentences in reading<br>• exploring ways of writing ideas, messages, in shortened forms, e.g. notes, lists, headlines, telegrams, to understand that some words are more essential to meaning than others<br>• making use of simple formats to capture key points, e.g. flow chart, 'for' and 'against' columns, matrices to complete in writing or on screen<br>• identifying intended audience i.e. self or others |
| **Term 3**<br>**T17** to 'scan' indexes, dictionaries and IT sources, etc. to locate information quickly and accurately<br><br>**T18** to locate books by classification in class or school libraries<br><br>**T19** to summarise orally in one sentence the content of a passage or text, and the main point it is making | **Term 3**<br>**T25** to revise and extend work on note-making from previous term<br><br>**T26** to summarise in writing the content of a passage or text and the main point it is making |

176

| READING COMPREHENSION | WRITING |
|---|---|
| **YEAR 4**<br><br>**Term 1**<br>**T17** to identify features of non-fiction texts in print and IT, e.g. headings, lists, bullet points, captions which support the reader in gaining information efficiently<br><br>**T23** to investigate how reading strategies are adapted to suit the different properties of IT texts, i.e. those which are scrolled and non-linear in structure; incorporate sound or still and moving images; can be changed; and have a spatial dimension | |
| **Term 2**<br>**T15** to appraise a non-fiction book for its contents and usefulness by scanning, e.g. headings, contents list<br><br>**T16** to prepare for factual research by reviewing what is known, what is needed, what is available and where one might search<br><br>**T17** to scan texts in print or on screen to locate key words or phrases, useful headings and key sentences and to use these as a tool for summarising text<br><br>**T18** to mark extracts by annotating and by selecting key headings, words or sentences, or alternatively, noting these | **Term 2**<br>**T21** to make short notes e.g. by abbreviating ideas, selecting key words, listing or in diagrammatic form<br><br>**T22** to fill out brief notes into connected prose<br><br>**T23** to collect information from a variety of sources and present it in one simple format, e.g. wall chart, labelled diagram |
| **Term 3**<br>**T20** to summarise a sentence or paragraph by identifying the most important elements and rewording them in a limited number of words | |

| READING COMPREHENSION | WRITING |
|---|---|
| **YEAR 5**<br><br>**Term 1**<br>**T23** to discuss the purpose of note-taking and how this influences the nature of notes made | **Term 1**<br>**T26** to make notes for different purposes, e.g. noting key points as a record of what has been said, listing cues for a talk, and to build on these notes in their writing or speaking<br><br>**T27** to use simple abbreviations in note-taking |
| **Term 2**<br>**T14** make notes of story outline as preparation for oral storytelling<br><br>**T16** to prepare for reading by identifying what they already know and what they need to find out<br><br>**T17** to locate information confidently and efficiently through (i) using contents, indexes, sections, headings (ii) skimming to gain overall sense of text (iii) scanning to locate specific information (iv) close reading to gain understanding (v) text marking (vi) using CDROM and other IT sources, where available;<br><br>**T18** how authors record and acknowledge their sources<br><br>**T19** to evaluate texts critically by comparing how different sources treat the same information<br><br>**T20** note-making: to discuss what is meant by 'in your own words' and when it is appropriate to copy, quote and adapt | **Term 2**<br>**T21** to convert personal notes into notes for others to read, paying attention to appropriateness of style, vocabulary and presentation<br><br>**T23** to record and acknowledge sources in their own writing |
| **Term 3**<br><br>**T16** note-making: to fillet passages for relevant information and present ideas which are effectively grouped and linked | **Term 3**<br><br>**T19** to construct an argument in note form |
| **YEAR 6**<br><br>**Term 1**<br>**T18** to secure the skills of skimming, scanning and efficient reading so that research is fast and effective | |

# Appendix 3: Effective letter writing

Letters are written for a broad range of purposes – to request action; to request (or provide) information; to describe an event; to express appreciation etc. The breadth of reasons for writing letters is also reflected in the range of text forms which letter writing covers, such as:

- *Recounts* e.g. a personal letter to a friend recounting a past event such as details of a holiday;
- *Explanations* e.g. a letter to a friend explaining an issue such as why they are thinking of becoming a vet;
- *Persuasion* e.g. a letter to a newspaper editor to persuade readers that, for example, a motorway's construction would have disastrous consequences for a local community.

When teachers have set up a letter writing activity which conforms to one of the above forms, they should refer to the relevant chapter in the book and adapt the Success Sheets as required.

## Layout of letters

All letters can be divided into two basic forms:
- Formal
- Personal

Formal letters are generally organised as follows:

1 Sender's address

2 Date of composition

3 Receiver's name and address

4 Formal greeting

5 Purpose paragraph

6 Expansions of purpose paragraph

7 Conclusion/summing up

8 Formal signing off

Personal letters omit the formality of the receiver's name and address, thereby reducing the number of basic components to seven.

The structuring of letters is best taught through the writing of real letters for real purposes with examples of the correct layout (included at the end of this appendix, pages 181–2 for photocopying and enlarging) displayed in the classroom as a visual reference. Teachers should note that it is now accepted that there should be no indenting. The layout of both formal and informal letters should be left hand justified. All breaks or divisions should be indicated by spacing.

## Audiences for letter writing

Writing letters for real purposes is, undoubtedly, the most effective way of teaching the art of letter writing. Possible audiences include authors and artists. Copies of *Who's Who?* or *Who's Who in British Art* may be found in local libraries and letters can then be sent direct to the author or artist at their home address. If a stamped addressed envelope is included, the number of replies increases markedly!

Teacher should observe the rule that it is *not* a good idea to send thirty or more copies of the same letter to one individual. The golden rule should always be: one letter written, one response expected. No one will reply to thirty members of a class!

Letters to newspapers also elicit a good response rate and, in the instance of 'Letters to the Editor' can provide a wealth of varied letter writing opportunities, e.g.
- responding to previous editorials/articles
- providing information on an issue of local interest or relevance
- agreeing (or disagreeing) with a feature story
- raising awareness about something happening in school
- clarifying the record in relation to an inaccurate or biased article previously published.

Two conventions should always be recognised if teachers encourage pupils to write to local papers:

1 Include both the school address and telephone number

2 Sign every letter.

## Letter writing and ICT

Teachers should note that many software packages bundled with computers include templates. Where templates for letter writing are included these may be used as an aid to teaching. ICT is certainly a great motivational tool for young writers and the opportunities which letter writing provides should not be missed. The modern equivalent of a pen-pal is also worth exploring – details can be found at www.epals.com

## Other forms of transactional texts

Other forms of transactional texts such as postcards, faxes and text messages also provide a real audience for writers and can be used in purposeful writing situations which augment the letter writing process.

# Layout of a formal letter

Sender's address            _____
                                                    _____
                                                    _____

Date of composition      _____

Receiver's name and address      _____

                            _____

                            _____

Formal greeting      _____

Purpose paragraph      _____

                            _____

                            _____

Paragraphs expanding purpose      _____

                            _____

1                             _____

2

etc.                         _____

                            _____

                            _____

Conclusion/ summing up      _____

                            _____

                            _____

Formal signing off      _____

                            _____

# Layout of a informal letter

Sender's address

_____

_____

_____

Date of
composition

_____

Informal greeting

_____

Purpose paragraph

_____

_____

_____

Extension of
purpose
paragraphs

1

2

etc.

_____

_____

_____

_____

_____

_____

Conclusion/
summing up

_____

_____

_____

Informal
signing off

_____

_____